THEN & NOW

LONG ISLAND CITY

Greater Astoria Historical Society
with Gary Vollo

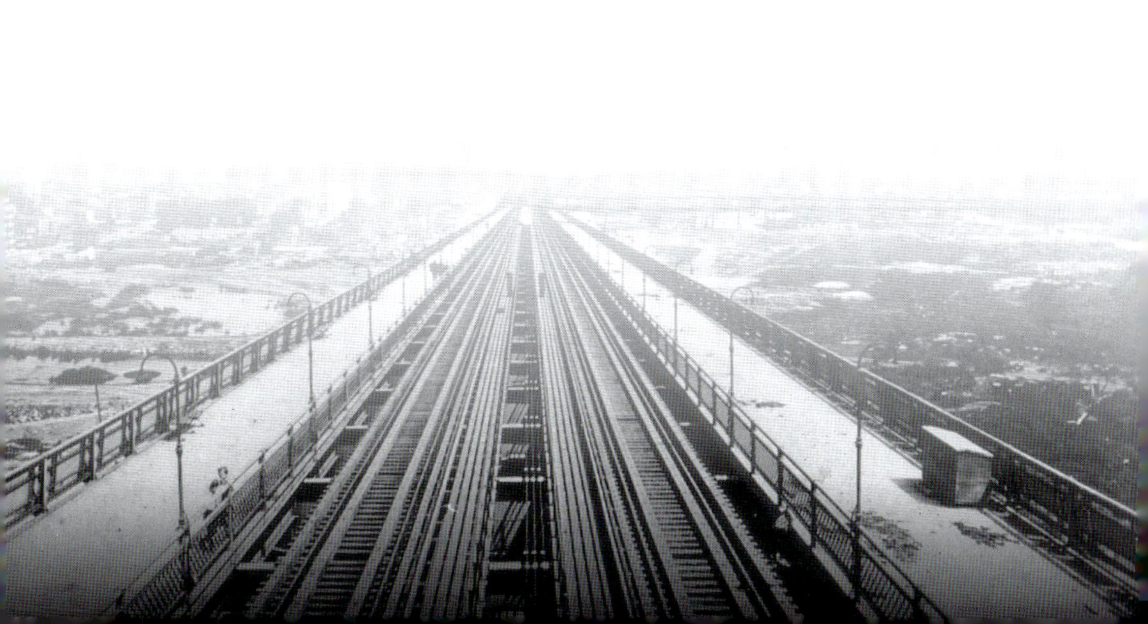

We dedicate this book to our Long Island City community. May we all learn not by our recollection of our past, but by the responsibility for our future.

ISBN 978-0-7385-7385-4

Library of Congress Control Number: 2010928218

Published by Arcadia Publishing
Charleston, South Carolina

Printed in the United States of America

For all general information, please contact Arcadia Publishing:
Telephone 843-853-2070
Fax 843-853-0044
E-mail sales@arcadiapublishing.com
For customer service and orders:
Toll-Free 1-888-313-2665

Visit us on the Internet at www.arcadiapublishing.com

On the Front Cover: St. Mary's Roman Catholic Church on Vernon Boulevard in Hunters Point is the heart of Long Island City. The leading proponent for incorporation as a city was Fr. John Crimmins, St. Mary's pastor. When a pro-city delegation went to Albany to push for legislation, Father Crimmins presented the governor with a "monster petition" that appeared to contain the signature of every man, woman, and child in Hunters Point. (Then photograph courtesy Greater Astoria Historical Society; now photograph courtesy Gary Vollo.)

On the Back Cover: More than three quarters of a century has passed since this photograph was taken, but with the exception of late-model cars, this view of 14th Place, looking north from 26th Avenue towards Astoria Park South, is virtually unchanged. Old Astoria Village is one of the most historically significant communities in New York City. Also see page 95. (Courtesy Greater Astoria Historical Society.)

Contents

Acknowledgments

Historians can navigate through archival images but fall short in the arena of contemporary images. This book would not be possible without the artistic talent of Gary Vollo. Gary, a native of Astoria, became interested in this particular project after seeing the neighborhood drastically altered with new, huge building complexes and the destruction of our neighborhood historic sites. Always the perfectionist, being part photographer and part archeologist, he was not satisfied until the modern image exactly replicated the historic one. This meant often going back to a site numerous times until even the traffic was in the right dimensions. Without Gary's involvement, this project might have come to a halt before it even started. He stated his goal for this project was to show how beautiful this area is and how, through the many transformations, it has maintained its elegance. Through his creative genius, Gary accomplished this goal.

Thank you to the many additional people who assisted with either photographs or in the production of this book: Bohemian Citizen's Benevolent Society of Astoria, Marie Carella, Iphegenia Fonazi-Kathefora, Donald Fedynak, Kaufman-Astoria Studios, Matt La Rose, Stephen Leone, the Mathews family, Richard Melnick, Queensborough Public Library–Long Island Division (John Hyslop and Erik Huber), Al Ronzoni, Vincent Seyfried, Bob Singleton, Henry Z. Steinway, Bob Stonehill, Sunnyside Chamber of Commerce, the Sunnyside Foundation, Constantine Theodosiou, Donna Van Blarcom, Debbie Van Cura, and Kevin Walsh.

Listed second, but providing equally invaluable encouragement to Gary Vollo, are Bruce Brooks for all his positive support and the assistance from Mary, Carol, and Anastasia Vollo.

A special thank you to Vincent Seyfried, whose classic book, *300 Years of Long Island City*, is the definitive resource for understanding the history of our community.

Last but not least, an enormous debt of gratitude goes to Robert Singleton of the Greater Astoria Historical Society for envisioning this project and being responsible for most of its research and writing. Bob is a true visionary leader who constantly challenges all of us, bringing out our best and leading us in a shared sense of purpose. With his eyes always on the horizon, he strategically finds a solution to every problem.

Unless otherwise indicated, the historic photographs in this book are from the archives of the Greater Astoria Historical Society. The modern images were all photographed by Gary Vollo.

For more information please visit our Web site at www.astorialic.org.

Introduction

Anthony Flint's book *Wrestling with Moses* chronicles the epic struggle between activist Jane Jacobs and developer Robert Moses. In one of Jacobs's arguments, she states, "cities are set in motion by planners and leaders but their flourishing was up to the people who inhabit them." Such words describe well both the creation and the success of Long Island City.

Its enviable location along the East River and Newtown Creek enabled Long Island City to adapt to changing realities from which its unique character would emerge. The need to link Manhattan with Long Island encouraged the formation of a string of roads and ferries along separate corridors. First traveled through by horsecar, later bus and rail lines were established to offer access to the developing region. Once this took shape, the area divided into three informal sections. The communities of Hunters Point, Blissville, and Sunnyside were connected with the ferry to Manhattan's 34th Street; Old Astoria Village and Steinway were joined with that which was located further north at 92nd Street. The middle portion of Ravenswood, Dutch Kills, and Astoria (and places with names now extinct, such as the German Settlement and Middletown) became the great residential and commercial center. This book's chapters reflect these three sections of Long Island City.

The communities came to exist in various ways, either through responsible speculation, enlightened corporate self-interest, or the effort of ordinary people linked by related occupation and background. Real estate speculators started Blissville, Ravenswood, and Astoria Village. Corporate interests were behind Steinway and Hunters Point. The German Settlement was a hamlet tied together by a group of people linked by occupation and background. Isolated by themselves, talk of unification rapidly grew.

The spark to unite these various hamlets was born as a popular revolution by those who dreamed of an opportunity to better their lives and those of their families. When Jane Jacobs wrote that "cities have the capacity of providing something for everyone, only because, and only when, they are created by everybody," she could well have had our community in mind. The urge to incorporate as a city, to provide services, and to pay for them themselves was a dream borne by people who lived here. In 1870, Albany gave this area a charter and a new identity: Long Island City.

However, the threat of bankruptcy nearly 30 years later would force the only indigenous city Queens ever knew to become a part of Greater New York in 1898. While this momentous occasion effectively put an end to Long Island City's cherished autonomy, its mettle was unaffected. To this day, the area's vitality lies not in politics but in its people, who never lost sight of what a better life meant for themselves and their families.

Long Island City's architectural legacy ranges from the colonial Lent-Riker-Smith House (presently the oldest private dwelling in New York City) to modern high-rise towers along the waterfront at Queens West. Distinctive—yet now endangered—high Victorian mansions have long defined Old Astoria Village, while Sunnyside Gardens, one of the first fruits of Greater New York's masterful early-20th-century urban plan, remains a standard of planned community living.

Degnon Terminal and its adjacent transportation infrastructure at Sunnyside Yards have defined Long Island City's utilitarian character for the greater part of the 20th century. When new, Degnon's industrial buildings were considered state of the art; their thoughtful design then still makes them useful and commercially desirable today.

Residents in Long Island City take enormous pride in how a range of familiar products has flowed over the years from their hardworking community to the far reaches of the globe: from Phelps-Dodge smelter and the petroleum products of Standard Oil's refineries to Pepsi-Cola, Chiclets Gum, and Dannon Yogurt. The old Paramount Studios (today's Kaufman-Astoria Studios) forever changed how people see the world. At the renowned Steinway Piano factory, artisans and craftspeople proudly adhere to their company's traditional emphasis on quality. It is a torch they carry with continued success.

For a final thought, Jane Jacobs states, "The point of cities is multiplicity of choices." Without question, this applies to Long Island City. Whether home for many with a vital stake in the American Dream, a thriving commercial area, or a cradle of creativity where artists and artisans come to fertilize one another's imagination, Long Island City stands out as a local neighborhood that embodies the many facets of the American spirit.

CHAPTER 1

Lower City

Hunters Point, Blissville, and Sunnyside

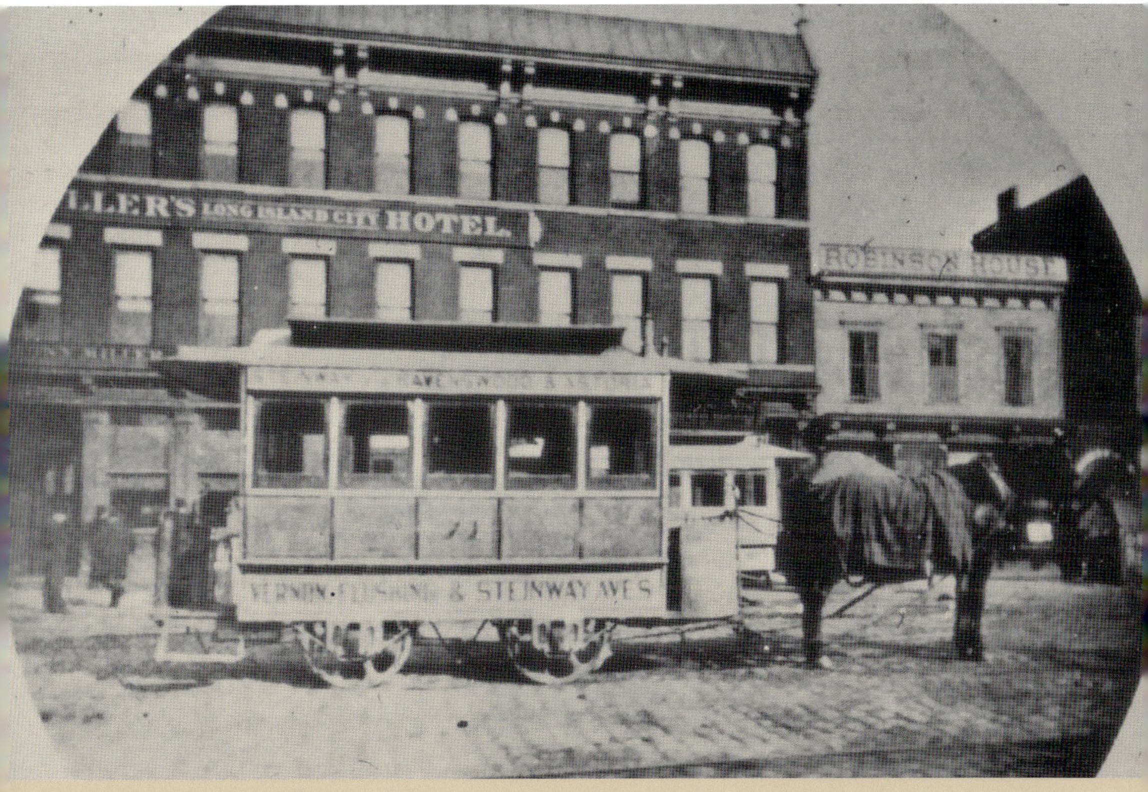

From 1870 to around 1920, a network of railroad and horsecar lines from Long Island and Queens converged at the 34th Street Ferry, which ran between Long Island City and Manhattan. Streetcar lines operated on Steinway Street, Vernon Boulevard, Astoria Boulevard, 31st Street, Borden Avenue, and Broadway. Miller's Hotel, in the background, was a famous saloon at the ferry. (Courtesy Vincent Seyfried.)

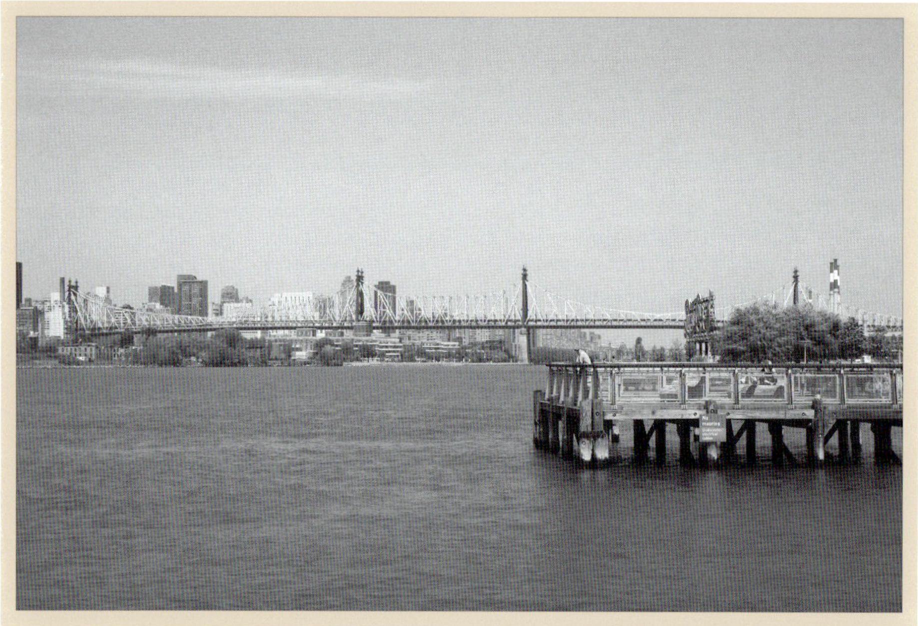

The Queensboro Bridge nears completion in 1908, spelling the death knell for Long Island City's role as a commuter hub. The last important commuter traffic shifted away when the new East River rail tunnel bypassed Hunters Point in 1910. Until mid-century, however, the waterfront remained a busy place for freight and manufacturing.

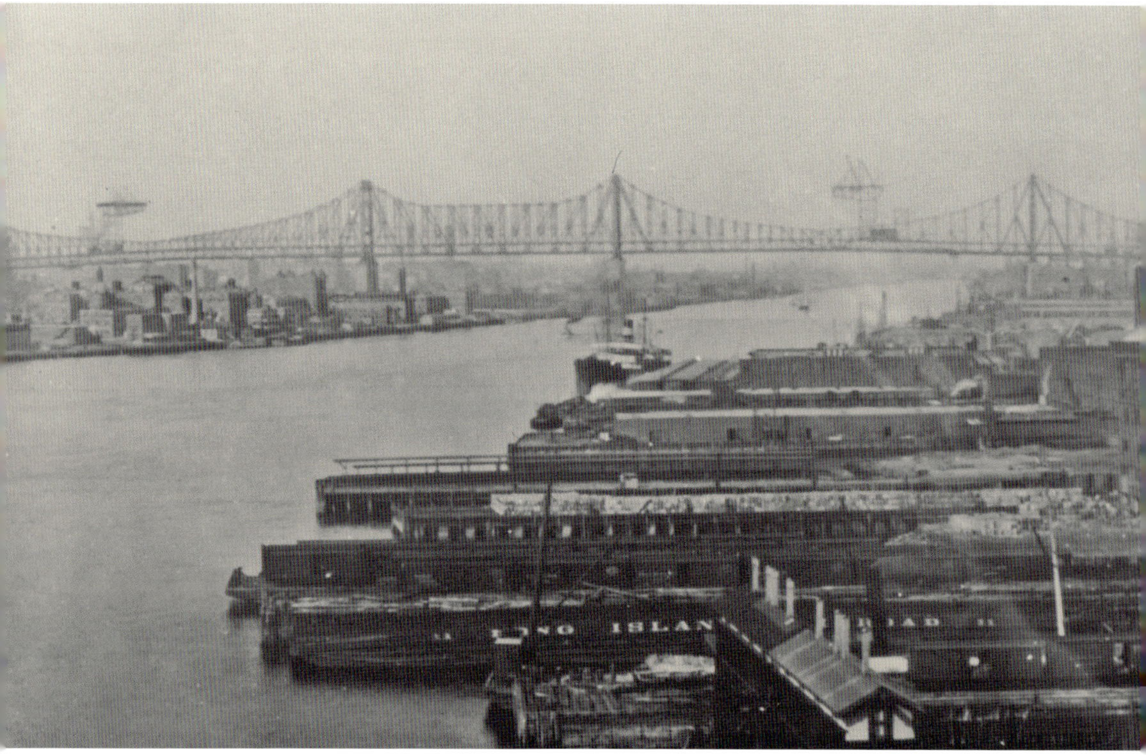

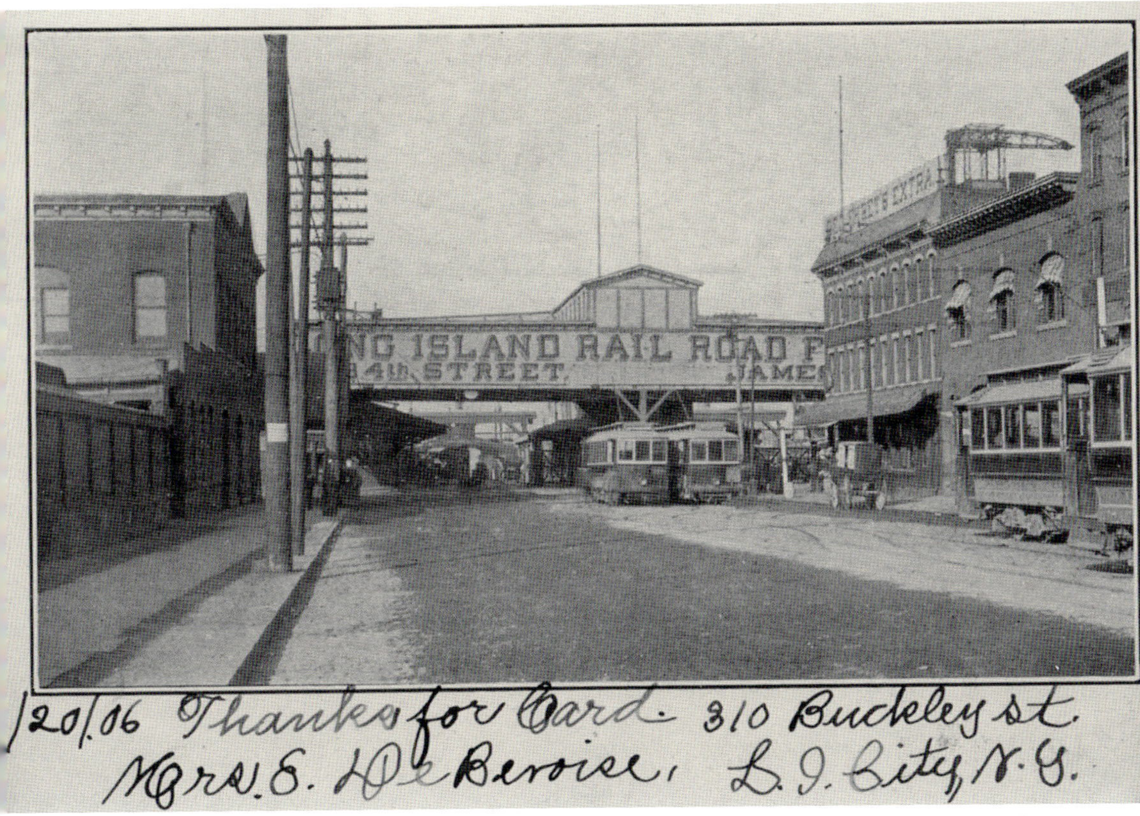

Seasoned patrons at the bar in Miller's Hotel (on the right) would time their last drinks with the warning bells that signaled a ferry's departure. To the left was the rail terminal, and in the center were the ferryboat docks. During the heyday of the East River ferries, this land was among the most valuable real estate on Long Island.

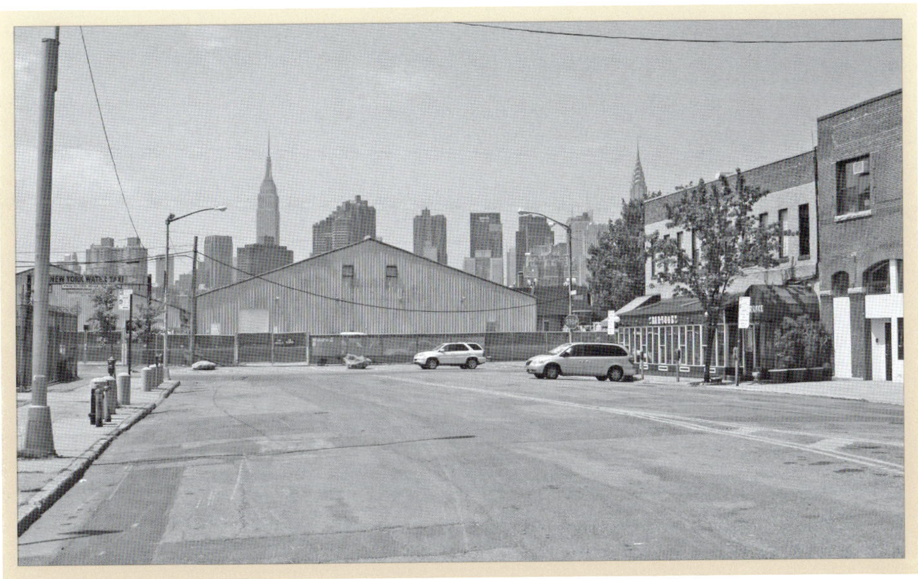

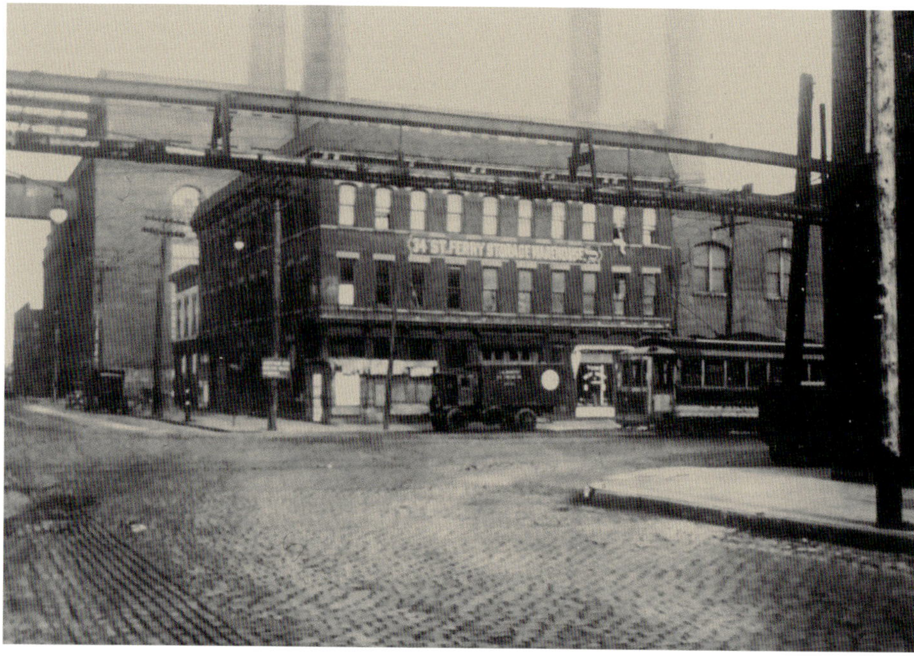

When commuters stepped off the ferry from Manhattan, McKim, Mead, and White's massive Pennsylvania Railroad powerhouse, its four stacks belching smoke, towered over the neighborhood. It was a reminder to the community that it owed its existence to the railroad. In the foreground is Miller's Hotel (today the Waterfront Crab House), with its three original stories. The ferry terminal is just off to the left in the photograph.

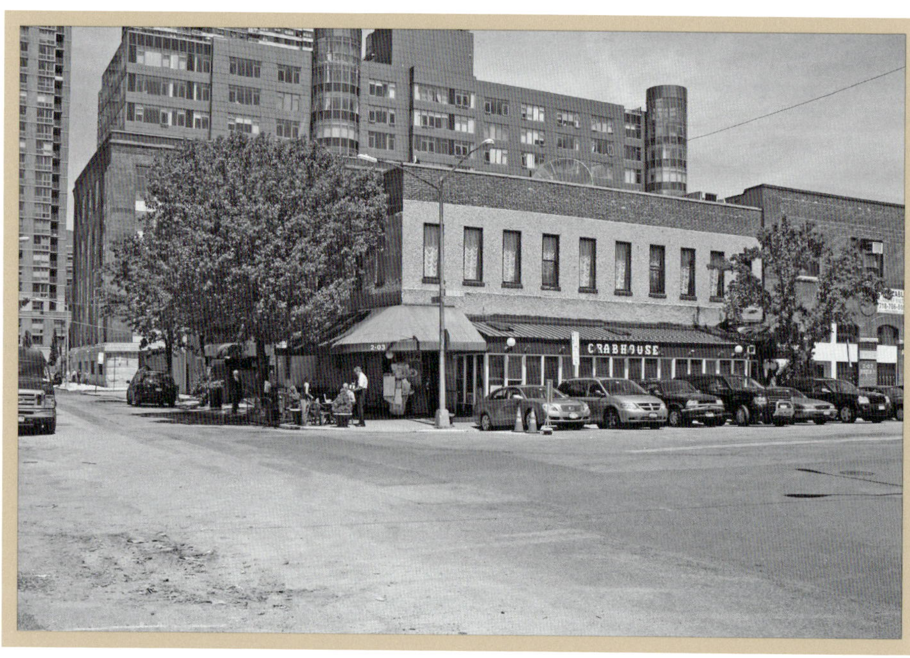

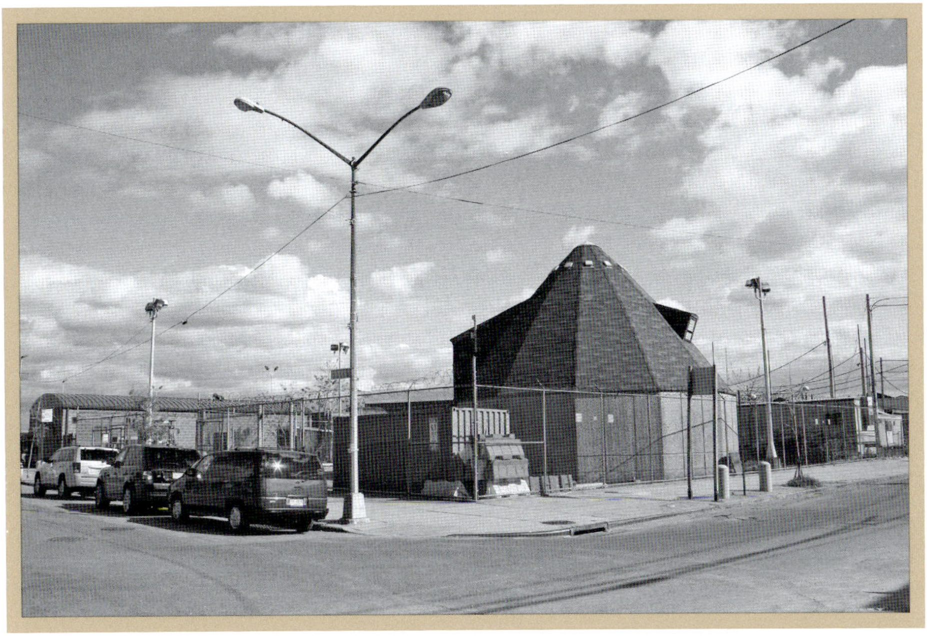

After it opened in 1859, boats docked twice an hour at the 34th Street Ferry in Hunters Point. It soon drew most East River traffic away from the older Astoria ferry to the north. Its importance only lasted a few decades. After the Queensboro Bridge (1909) and Penn tunnels (1910) opened, annual ferry traffic fell from 6 million to less than 1,000 by 1918. The ferry was shut down in 1925, and the railroad terminal, pictured below, closed.

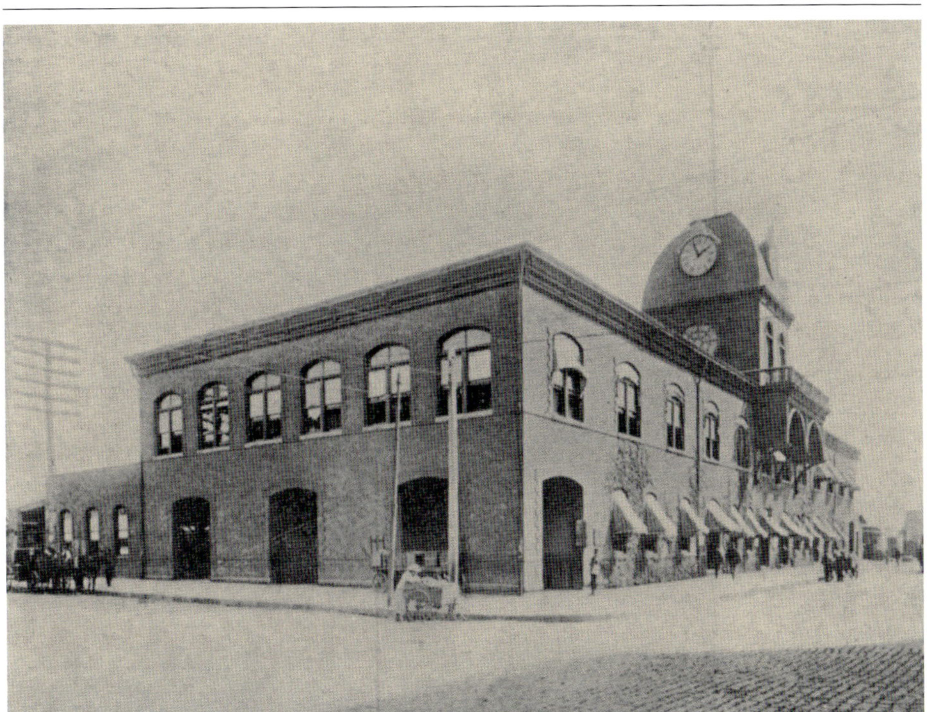

The Pennsylvania Railroad powerhouse supplied electricity to the railroad from New Jersey to Queens, including Penn Station and the Sunnyside Yards. The plant sits on a concrete slab 6 feet thick and is supported by more than 9,500 piles driven into the marsh. Four 275-foot smokestacks vented smoke from 64 coal-fired boilers. The plant was designed to make electricity by producing steam that drove turbines. It was obsolete by the 1920s. The building was recently converted into condominiums. The stacks were taken down in 2005. (Then photograph courtesy Stephen Leone.)

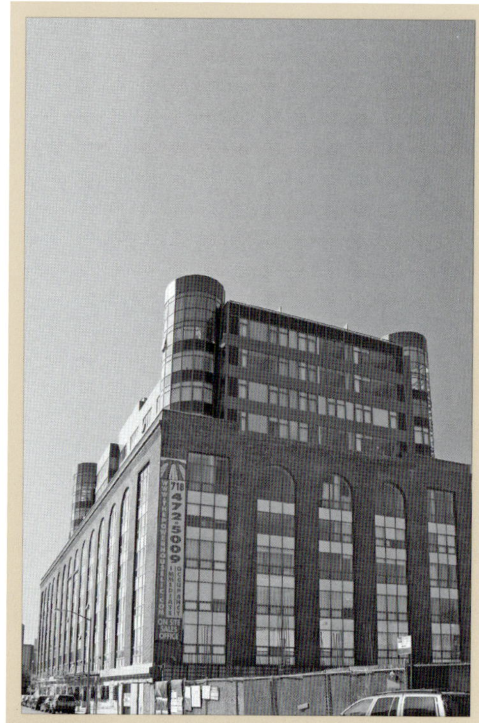

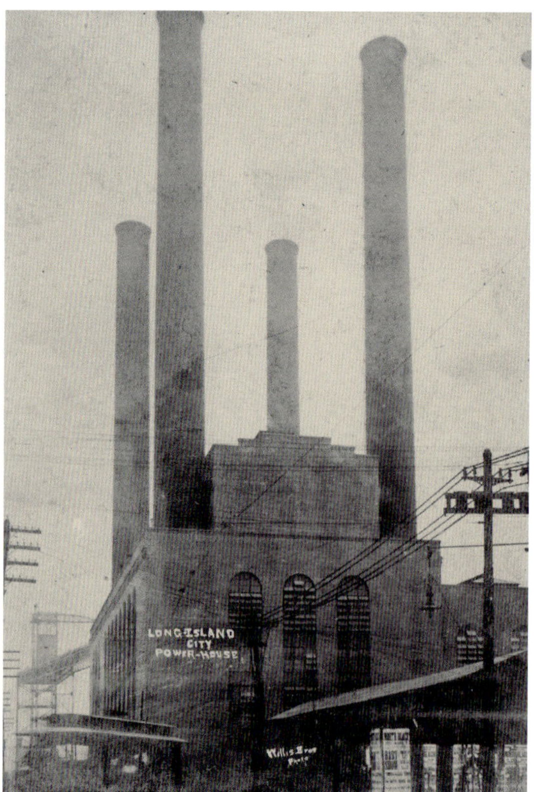

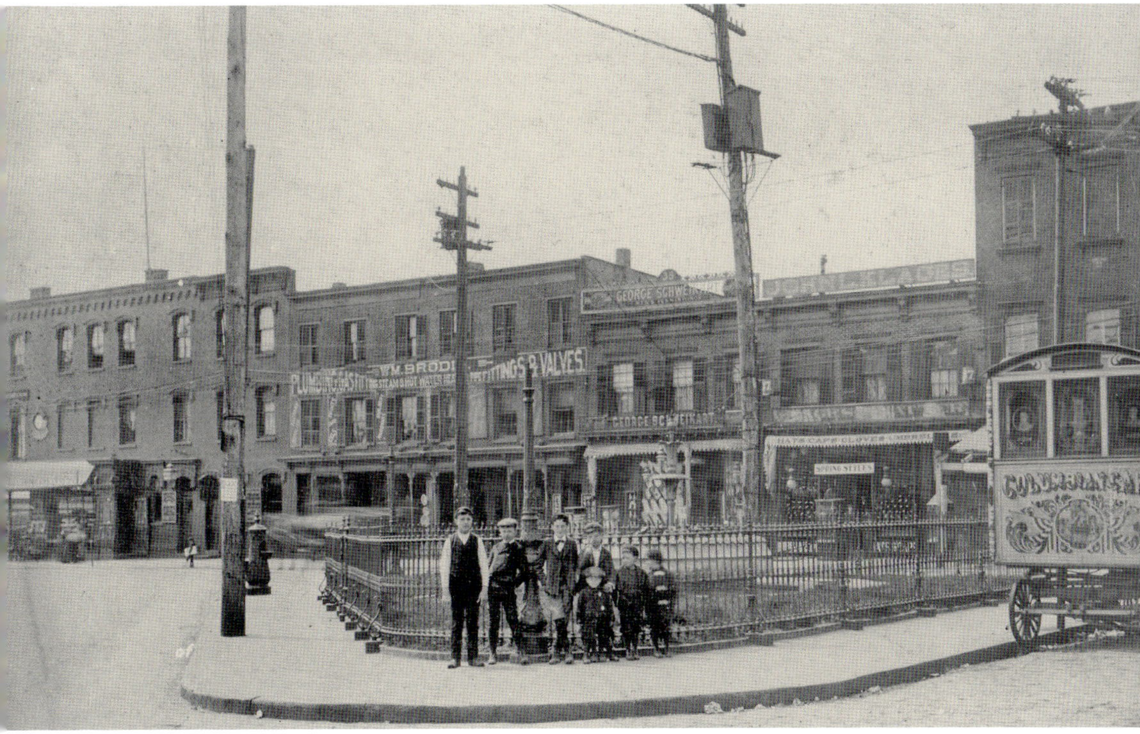

This is looking west at Monitor Square, the city center for commerce and business. The square was laid out in the early 1860s and was so named because its long and narrow shape resembled the Civil War ironclad. Vernon and Jackson Avenues met here, just east of the ferry terminal. The historic image shows a fountain within the square and a lunch wagon. The seven people give the picture its caption "The Monitor Seven."

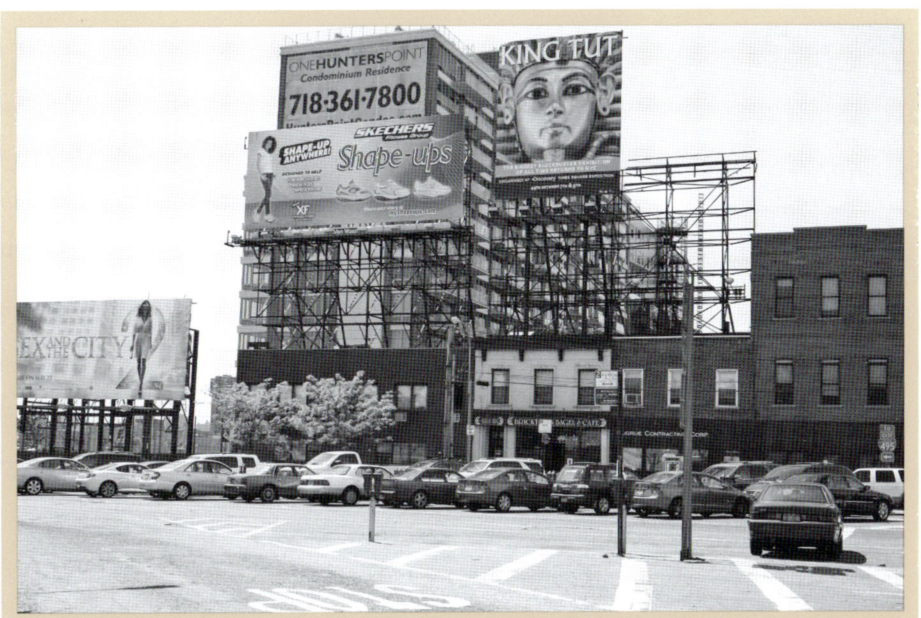

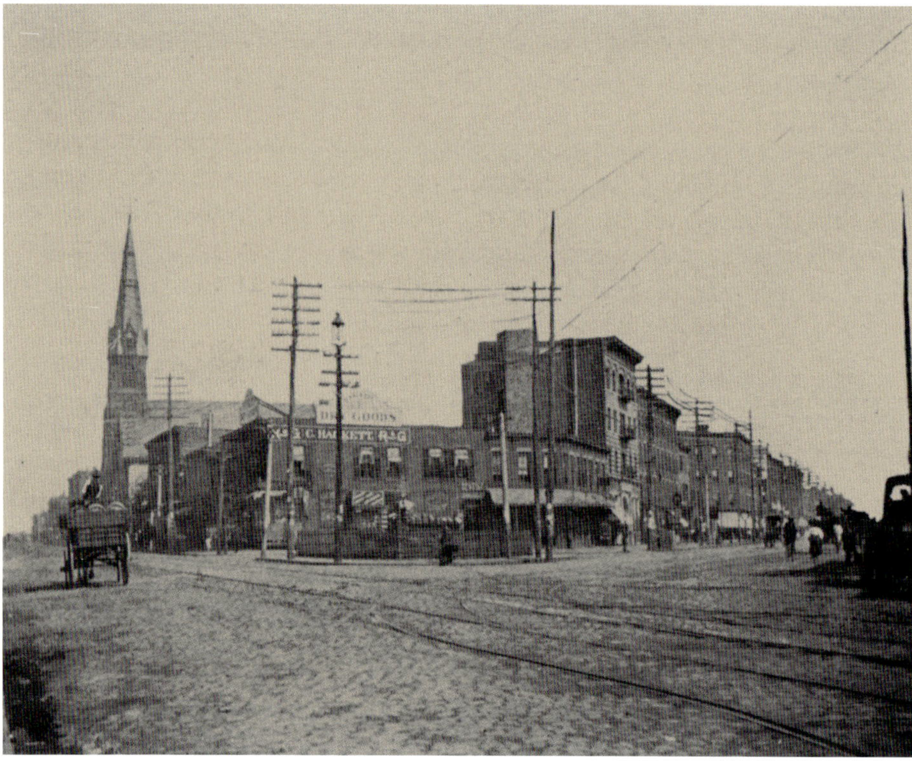

Monitor Square is pictured again, this time looking north. The road on the left, past St. Mary's steeple, is Vernon Boulevard, the road to Astoria, built by the Ravenswood, Hallett's Cove, and Williamsburgh Turnpike and Bridge Company (1838). On the right is Jackson Avenue, formerly the Hunter's Point, Newtown, and Flushing Turnpike (1857), which is, as its name implies, the road to Flushing.

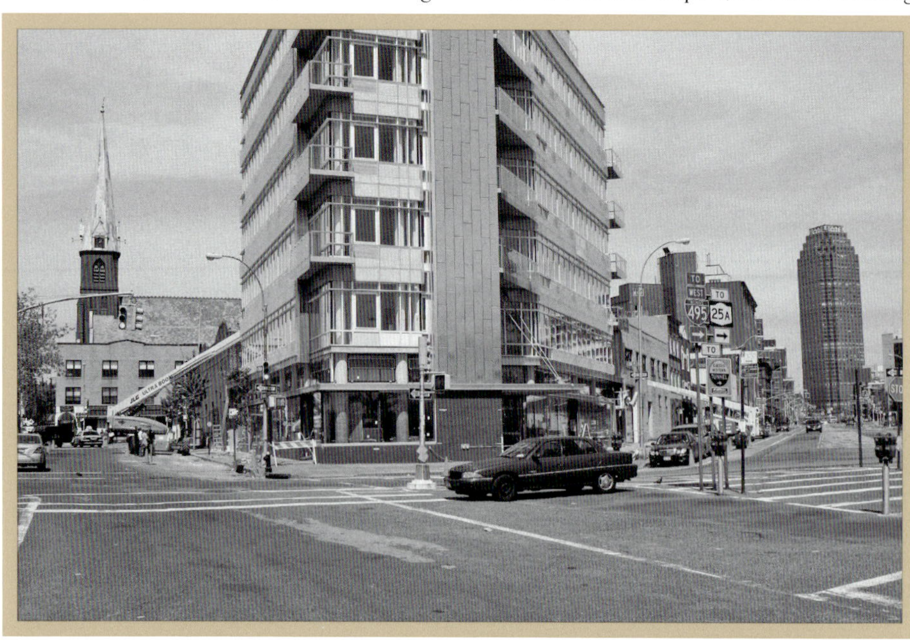

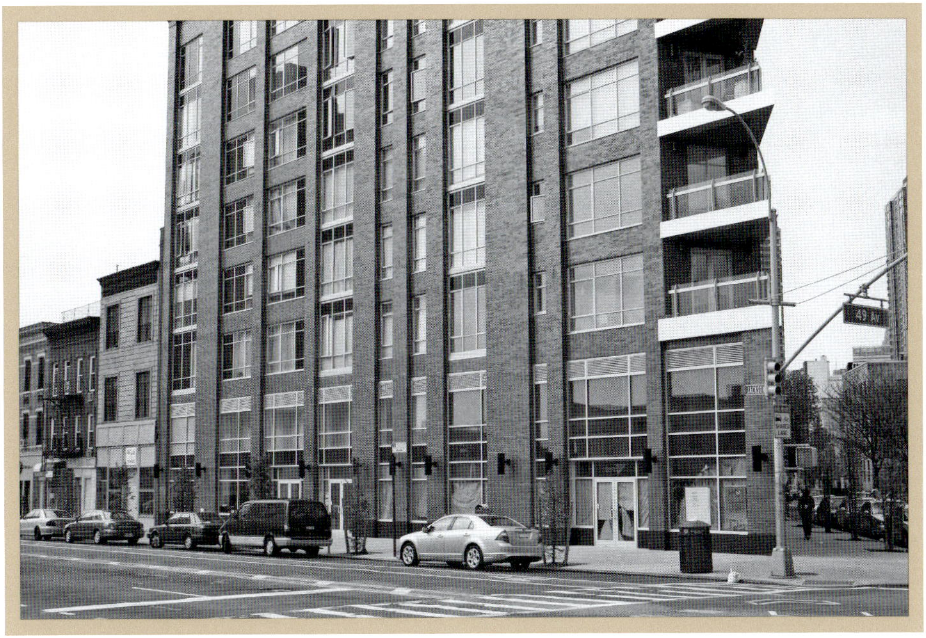

The Hackett Building at 10–63 Jackson Avenue was opened in the 1890s by O. Demarest, a dry goods merchant, as the first department store in Queens. After the consolidation of the five boroughs into New York City (1898), it was the first Queens Borough Hall. Efforts to designate the building a landmark failed, and it was destroyed in 2007 to build a large condominium.

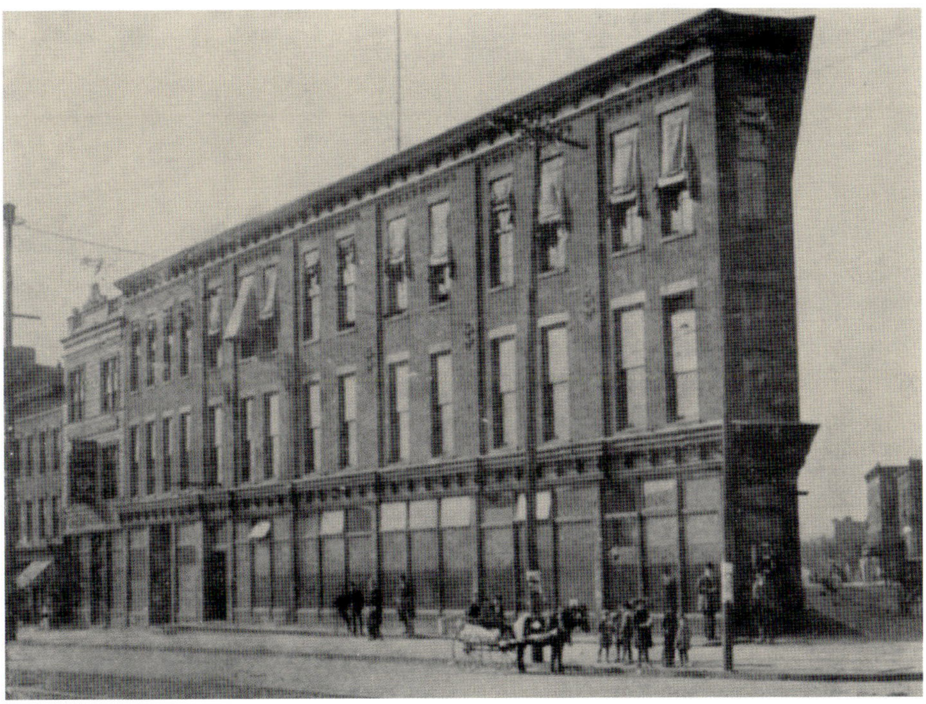

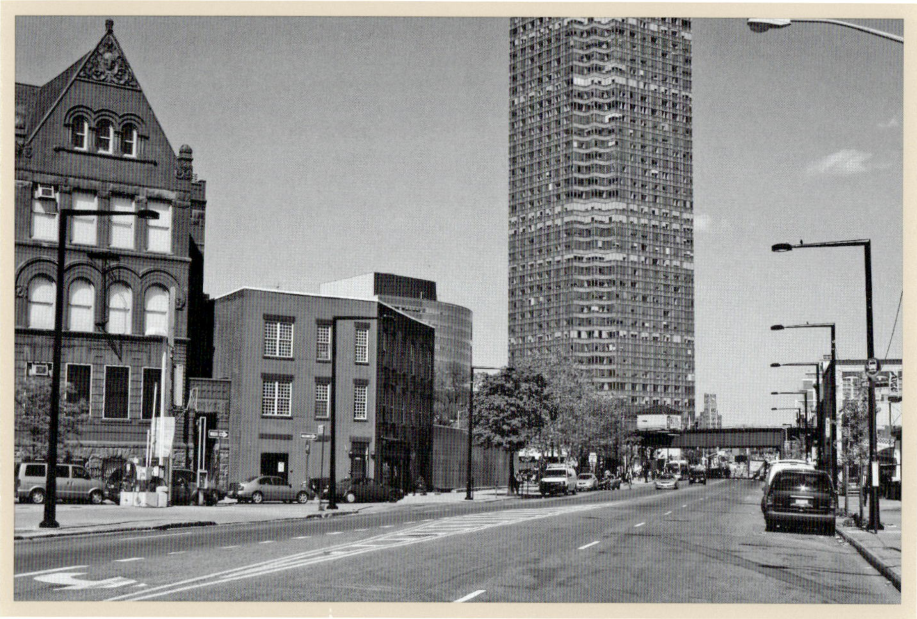

This view of Jackson Avenue looking north shows the buildings between P.S. 1 (left) and St. John's Hospital (center). It was the main street for the bustling midsized metropolis. The modern image shows the Citicorp Building, which has replaced St. John's Hospital. It is the tallest building between Manhattan and Boston.

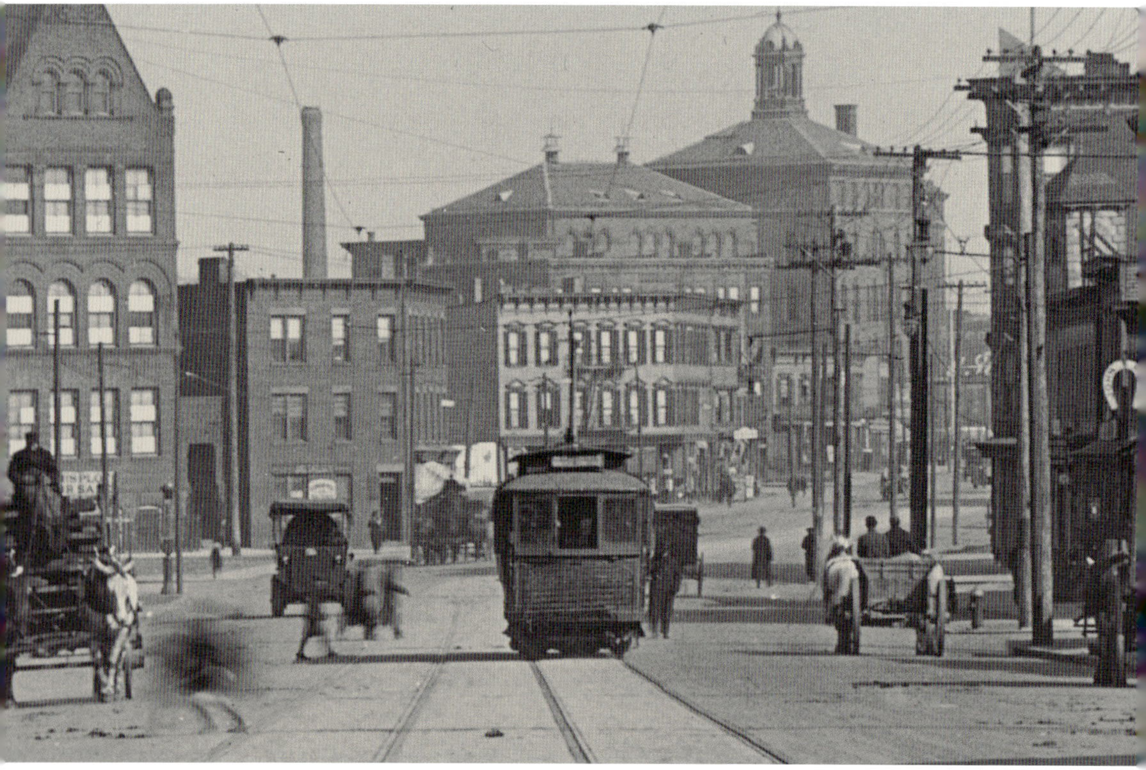

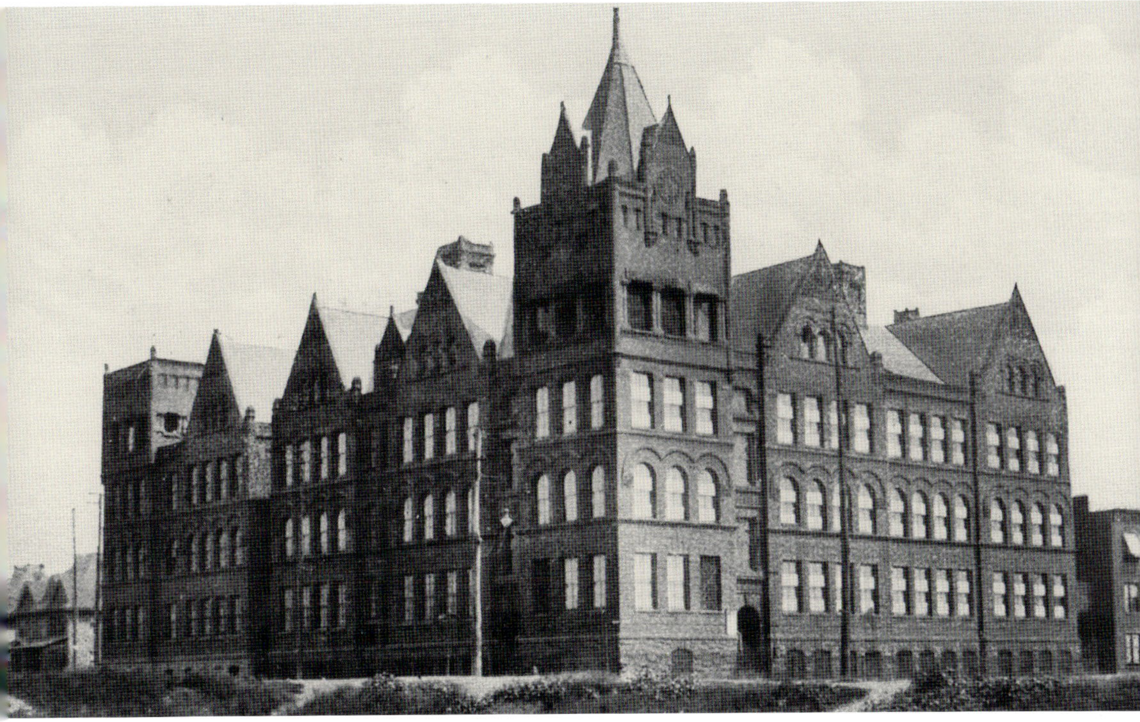

P.S. 1, with a one-time enrollment of 2,500 students, was the largest public school on Long Island. Mayor Patrick Gleason of Long Island City, who pushed for its completion in 1892, considered it his gift to the community's youth. It later suffered low attendance and was closed in the early 1960s. It reopened in 1971 as an artist workspace and gallery now styled as MoMA P.S. 1. The corner bell was removed after a fire. (Then photograph courtesy Gary Vollo.)

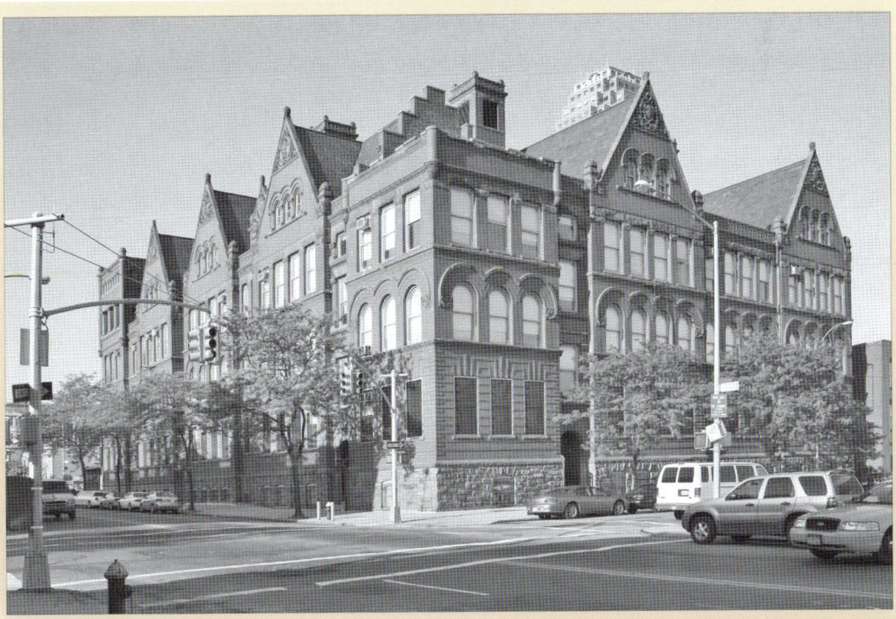

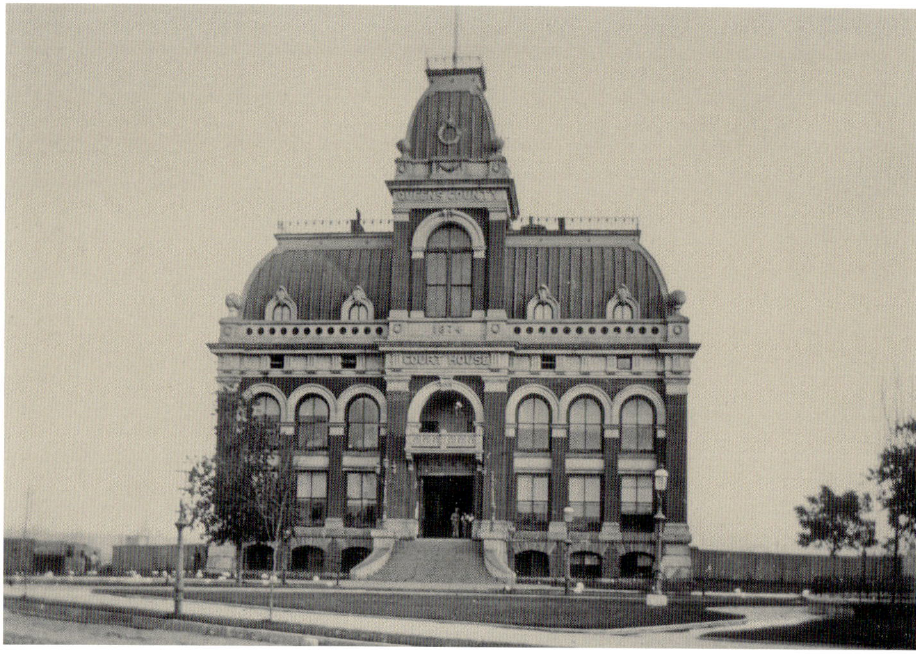

The county seat and courthouse for Queens County (which then included Nassau County) moved in 1874 to Long Island City. The building was plagued by a chronic leaky roof. One of the many efforts to remedy the problem started a fire that destroyed it in 1904. The second courthouse, completed in 1908, is still used by the Queens County Supreme Court.

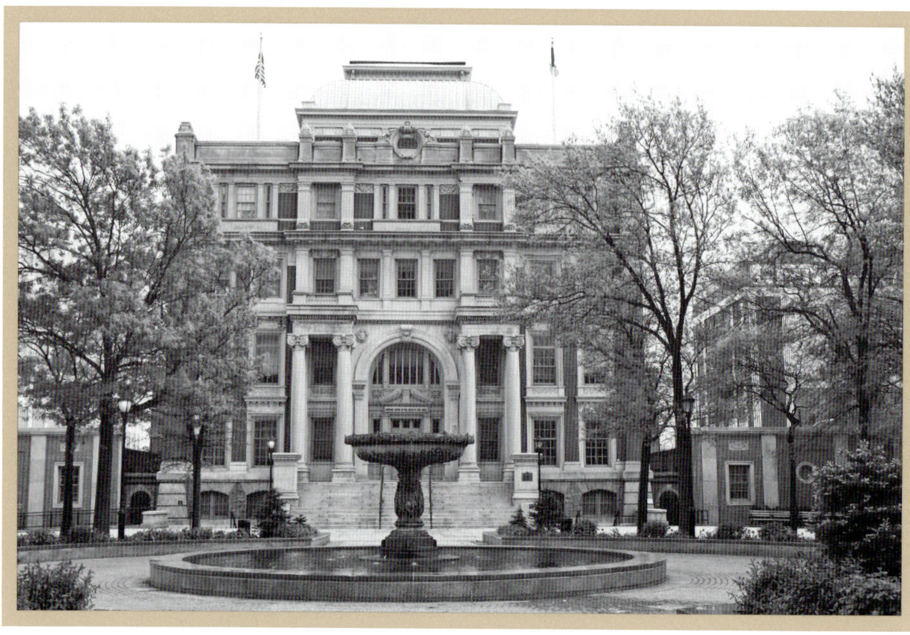

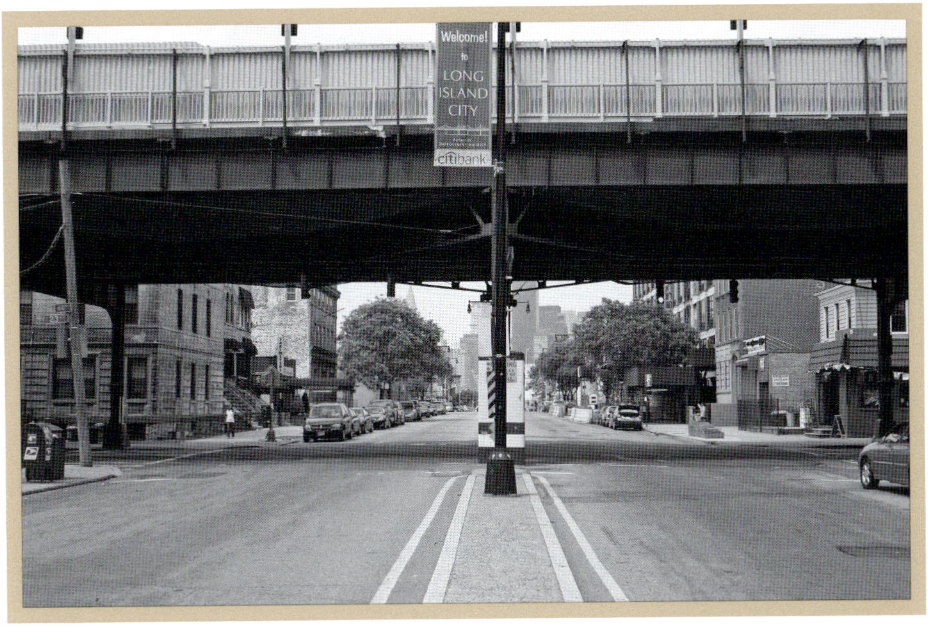

With a manicured median down the middle of the street, Nott Avenue (today 44th Drive) was one of the more attractive blocks in Hunters Point. Prosperous residents lived in its homes and apartments. They bitterly opposed a suggestion by the city in 1913 to route an elevated line through the block, fearing that the elevated tracks would lower property values and disturb patients at nearby St. John's Hospital.

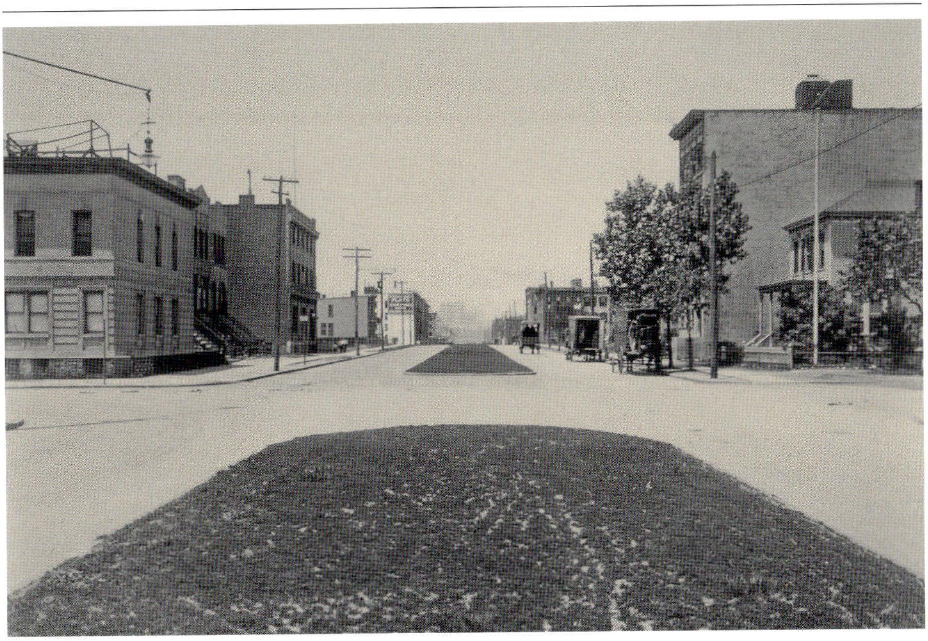

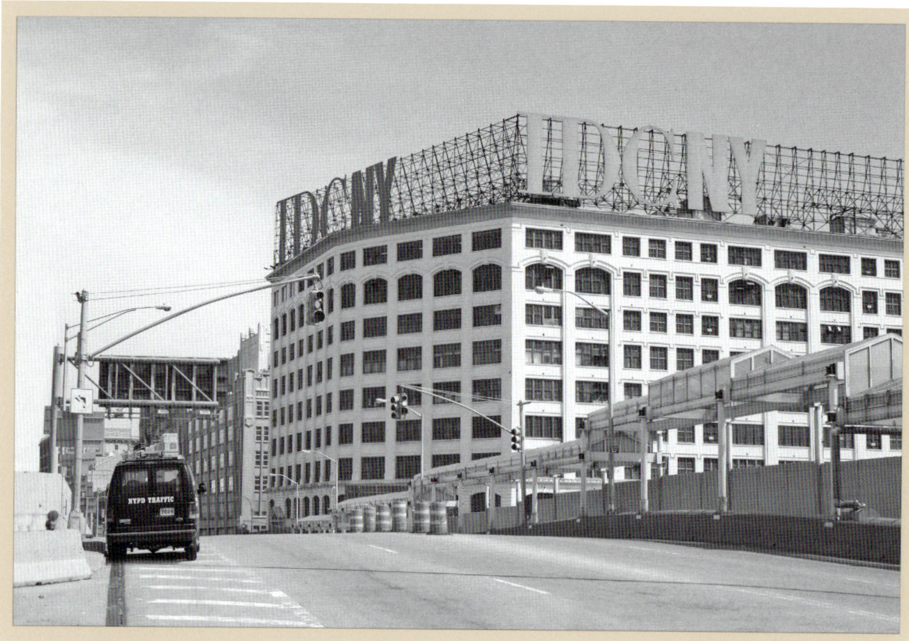

The "Thousand Window Bakery" of Loose-Wiles Sunshine Biscuits was once the largest employer in Long Island City with a payroll of 2,400. It was the flagship for Degnon Terminal, a 125-acre industrial park that gave potential tenants access to both water (Dutch Kills) and rail (Sunnyside Yards) transportation. Opened in 1905, the factories and warehouses had large windows for light and ventilation. The Sunshine Biscuit Building is now part of the campus of La Guardia Community College.

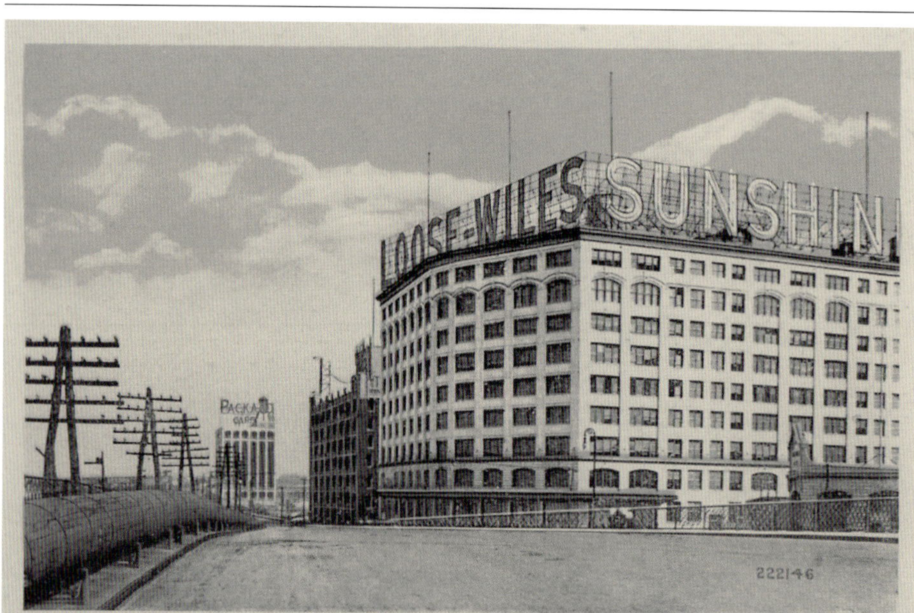

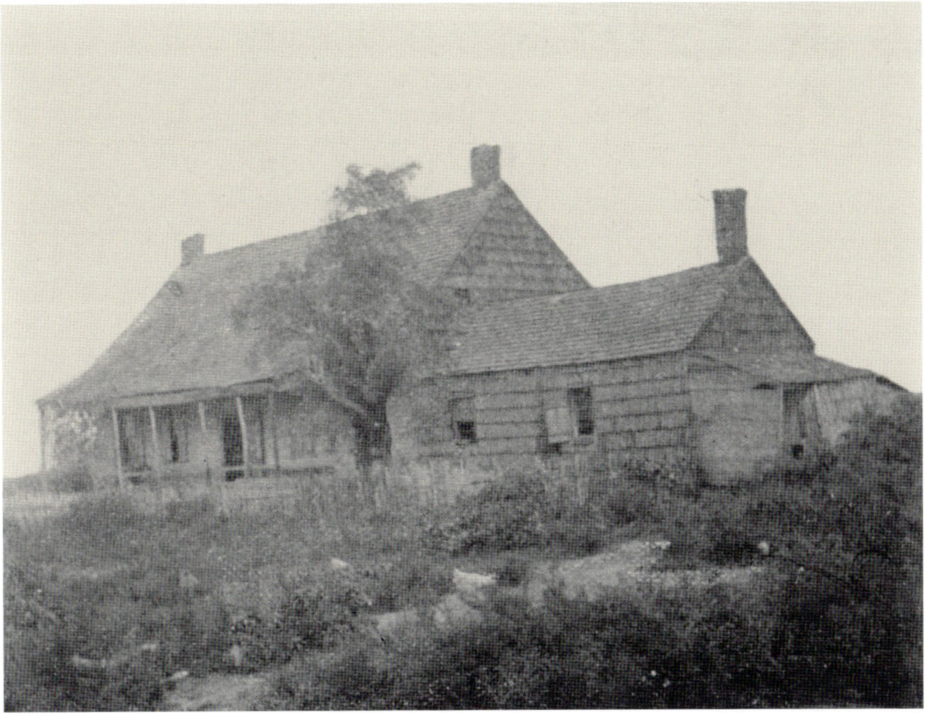

From the earliest European settlement along Newtown Creek and Dutch Kills, a number of ancient buildings lingered into the first decades of the 20th century. Commercial development and residential construction quickly swept them away. Lacking modern amenities such as running water and sewers, their passing was, for the most part, unmourned. Near this traffic island at Van Dam Street and Borden Avenue was the mid-17th-century Duryea House.

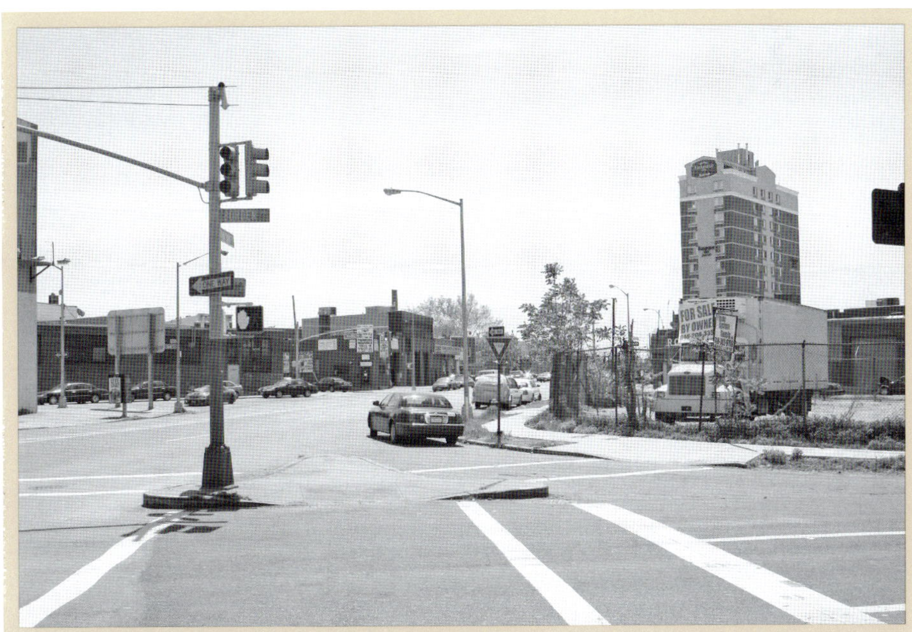

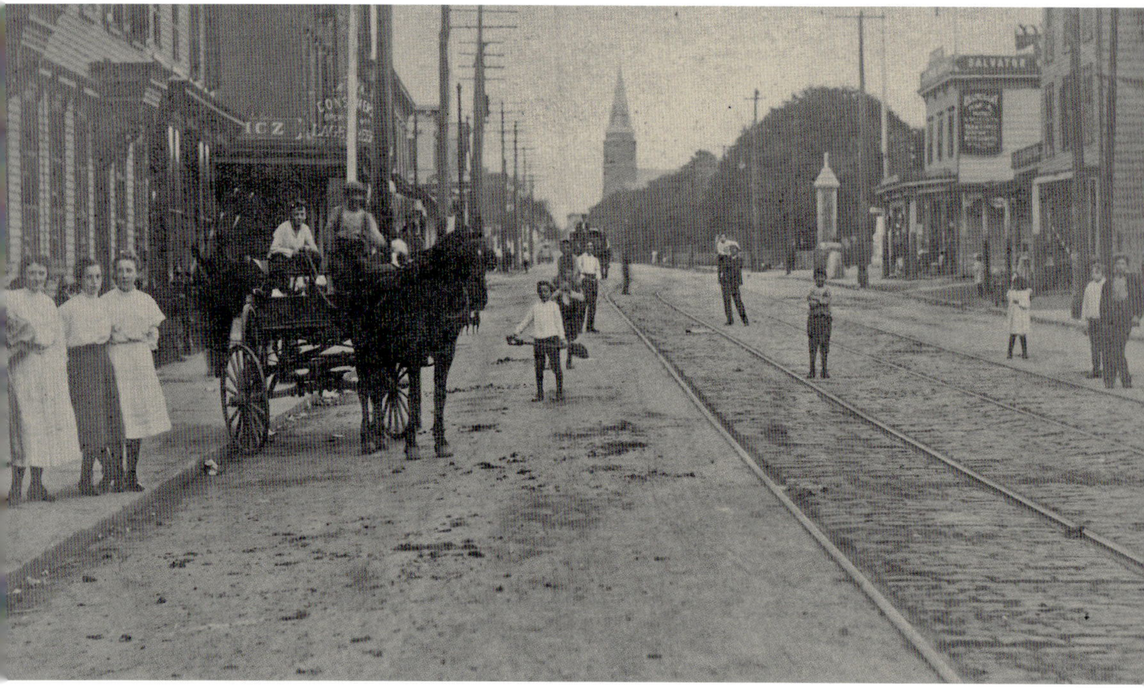

A wealthy Brooklynite, Neziah Bliss made his fortune building steam engines and steamboats, as well as in real estate ventures. He created Brooklyn's Greenpoint community and started the hamlet of Blissville across Newtown Creek in Queens. By the 1830s, he opened Greenpoint Avenue, the main street of Blissville. He bridged Newtown Creek and continued the road to Woodside. In the background are the trees of Calvary Cemetery and the steeple of St. Raphael's Roman Catholic Church. (Then photograph courtesy Bob Stonehill.)

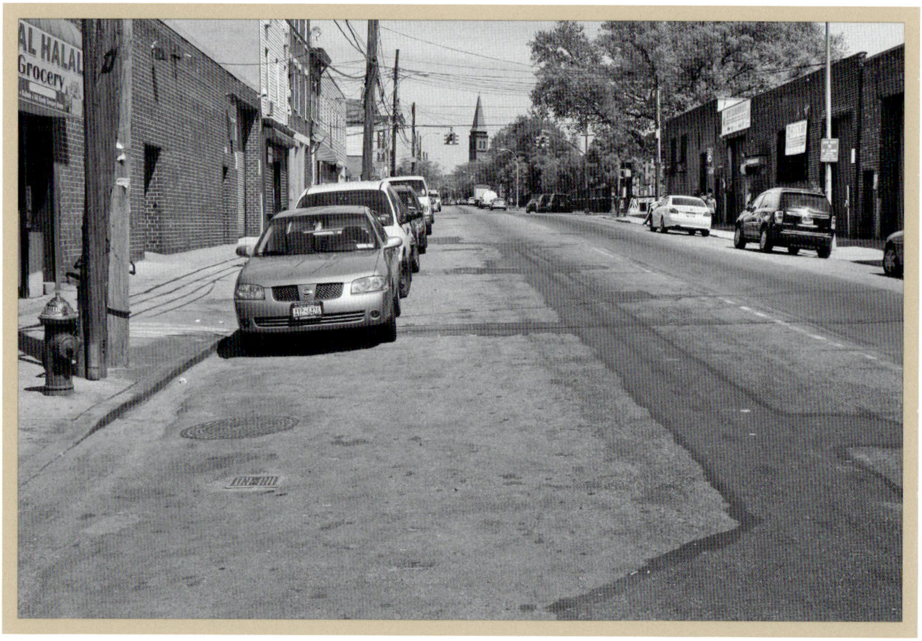

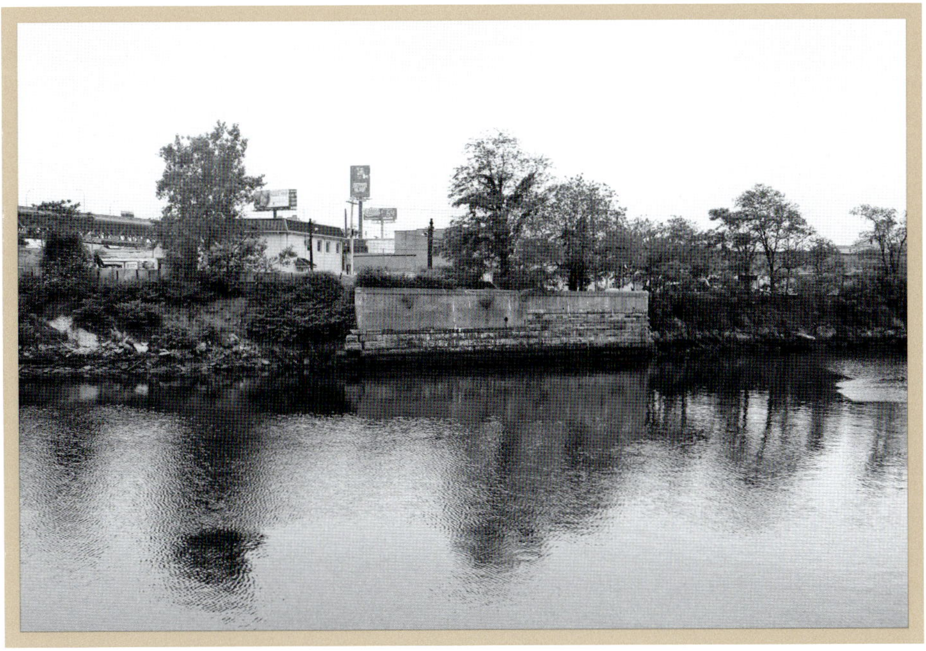

In the 17th century, Humphrey Clay, a supposed associate of pirate Captain Kidd, started a ferry over Newtown Creek linking Maspeth and Greenpoint, Brooklyn. After Calvary Cemetery opened (1848), a number of years passed before horsecar lines reached it. Penny Bridge, on the Bushwick and Newtown Turnpike, was the easiest route to the cemetery from the Brooklyn ferries. The toll was removed in 1878, and the massive Kosciuszko Bridge replaced the older bridge in 1939.

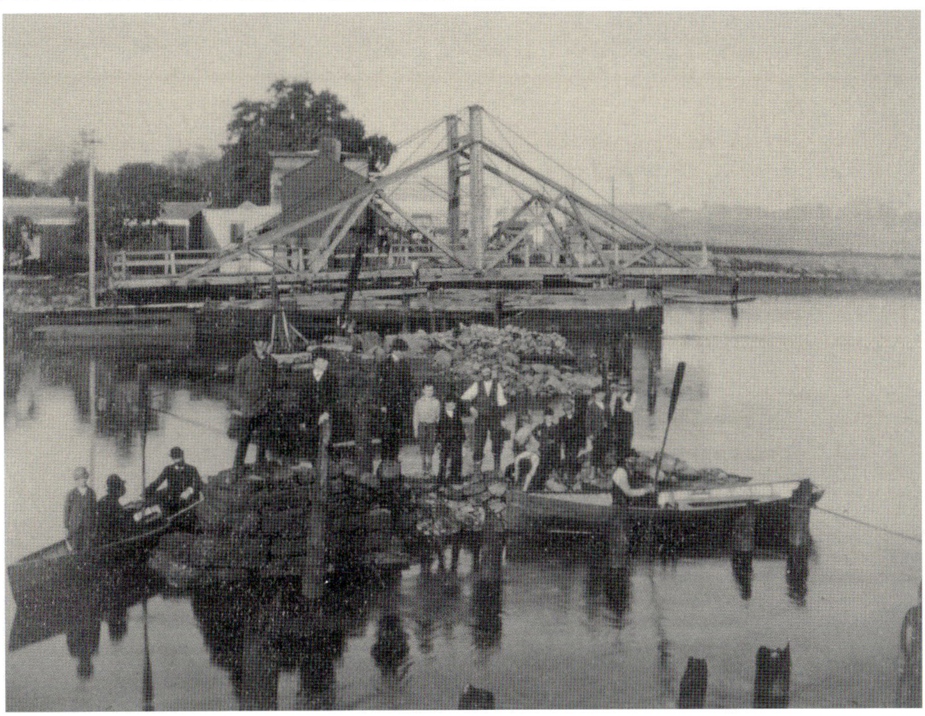

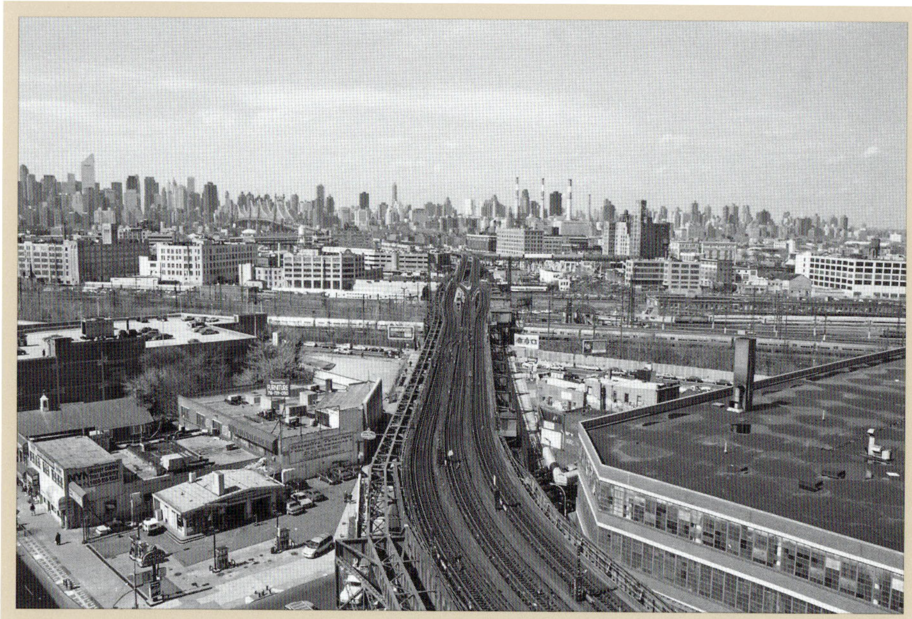

Dutch Kills was once a marshy backwater. In the span of a decade, it became not only the borough's business center at Queens Plaza, but also, with Sunnyside Yards, a regional transit hub. When a bridge over the rail yards linked Queens Plaza (and the Queensboro Bridge) to Queens Boulevard, the span over the East River realized its full potential with direct access to every corner of the borough. The bridge traffic included some of the busiest streetcar and elevated train lines in the city. This photograph is from the roof of the former Packard Building.

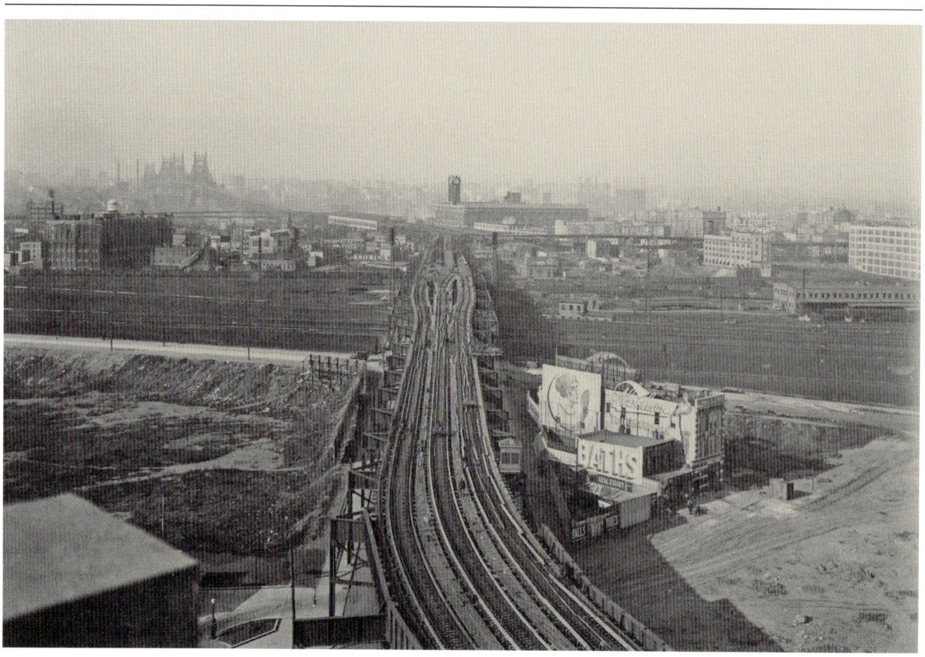

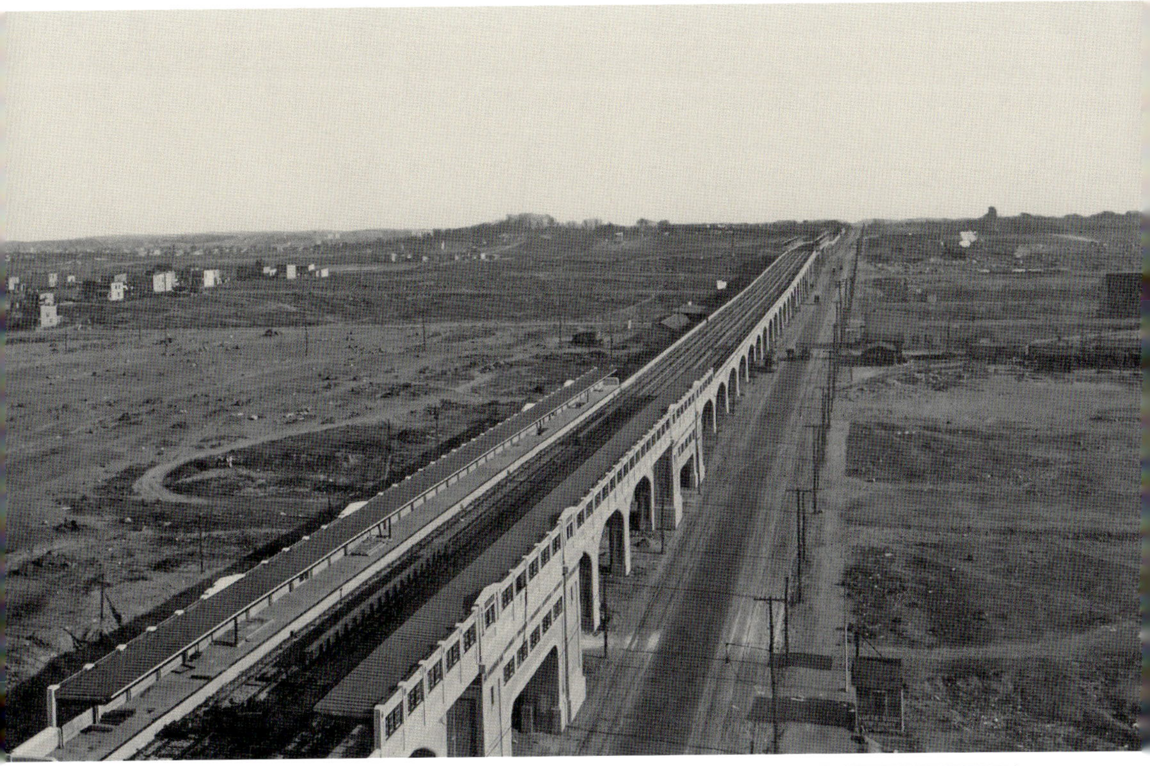

Once called Long Island City Heights or the Blissville Ward, Sunnyside was sparsely settled until the elevated line opened in April 1917. Manhattan (and Astoria or Corona) was but 15 minutes away. The blocks were filled, virtually overnight, with excellent examples of all types of housing, from model flats and planned communities to apartment buildings of every scale and single-family homes. Many residents characterize Sunnyside as one of the city's finest communities. This view is also from the Packard Building roof, this time looking east.

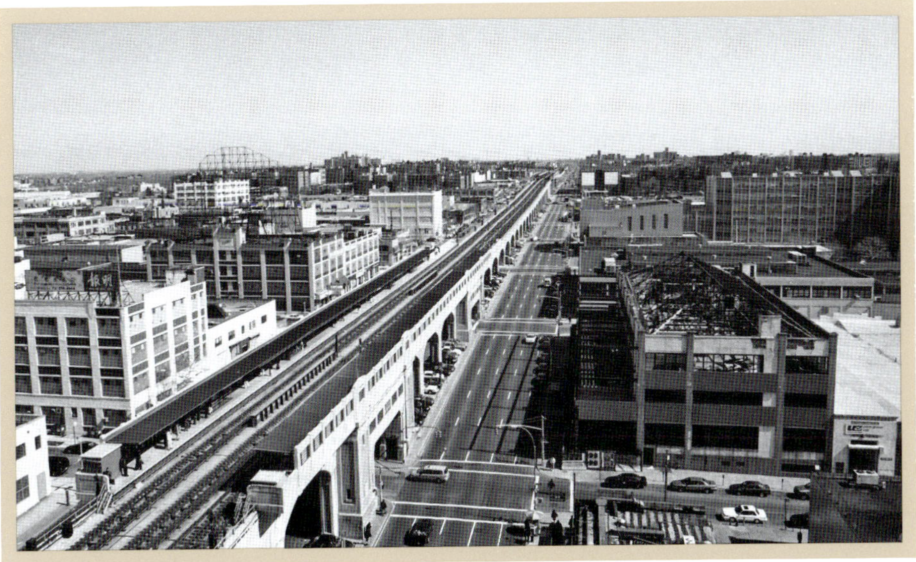

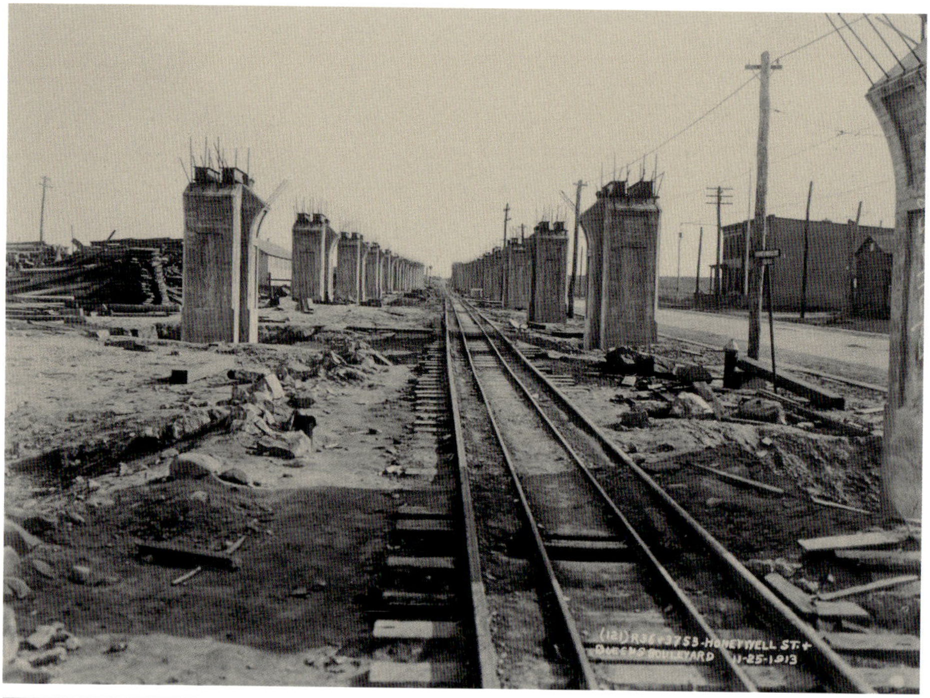

A European-style viaduct runs over Queens Boulevard, making the Sunnyside section unique in the New York City transit system. The tracks are enclosed in a concrete structure that muffles train noise. Underneath the arches once ran streetcar tracks, which gave way decades ago to parking for cars. At one station, Lowery (today 40th) Street, annual ridership went from 77,000 in 1920 to nearly 2 million by 1929. This is from 35th Street looking east.

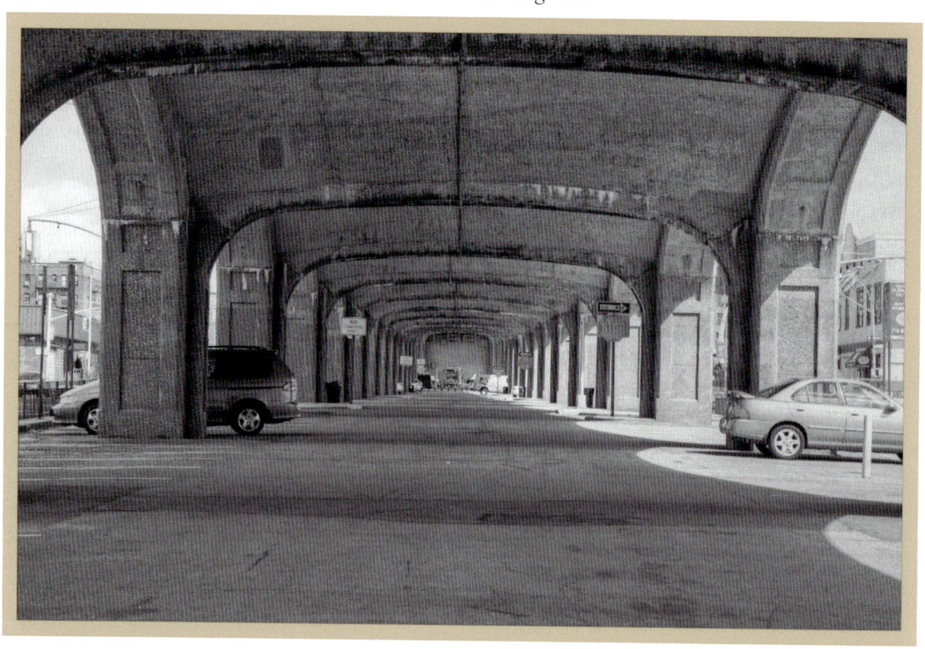

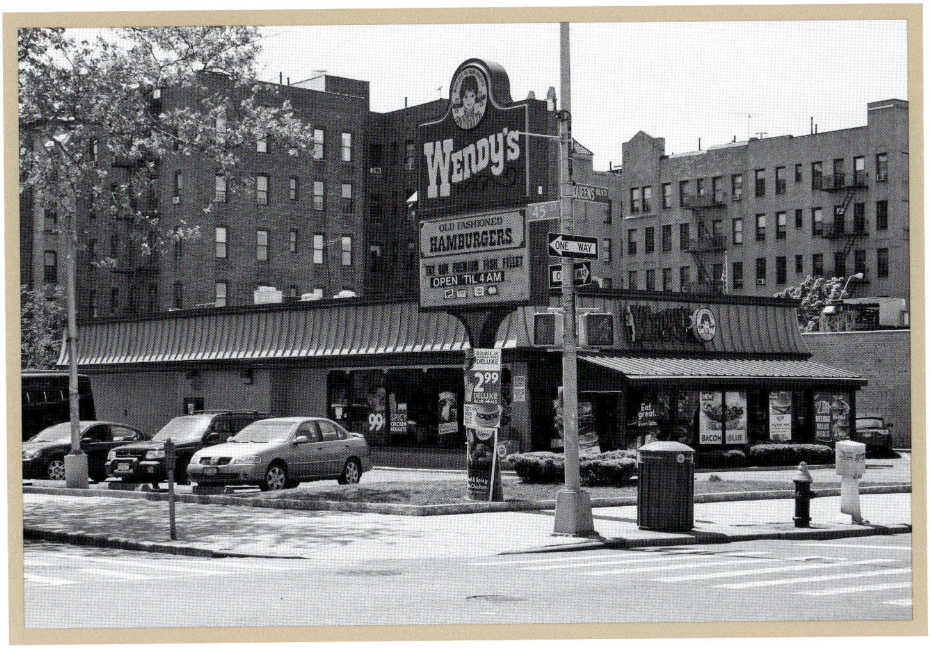

Sunnyside Garden Arena, formerly at Queens Boulevard and 45th Street, was a private tennis club in its early days. Between 1945 and 1977, during the early days of television, it gained fame as a venue for boxing and wrestling matches. While campaigning for president in 1960, John F. Kennedy made a stop here. The building, a significant cultural landmark, was replaced by a hamburger outlet.

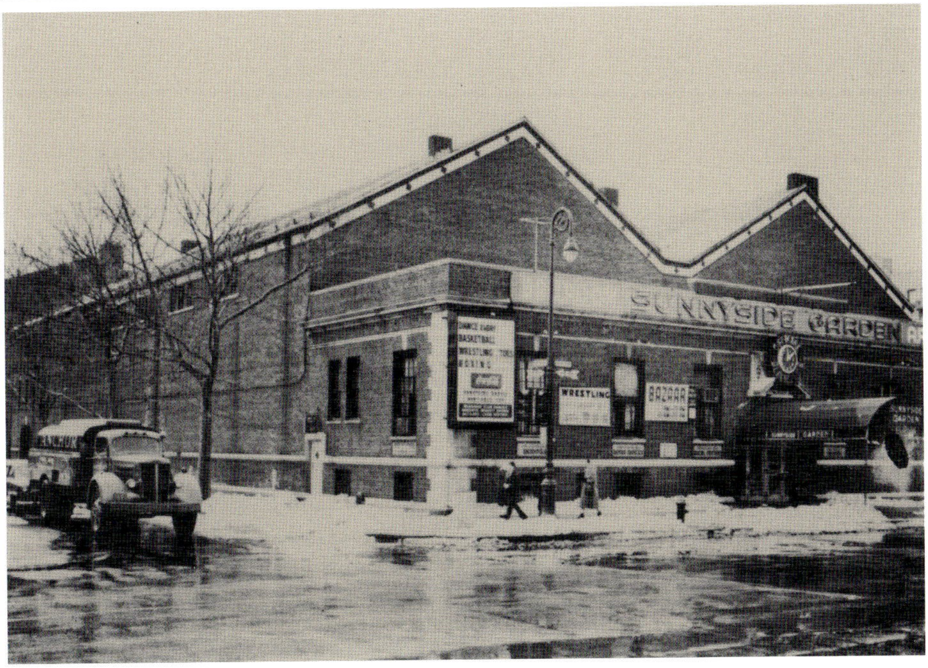

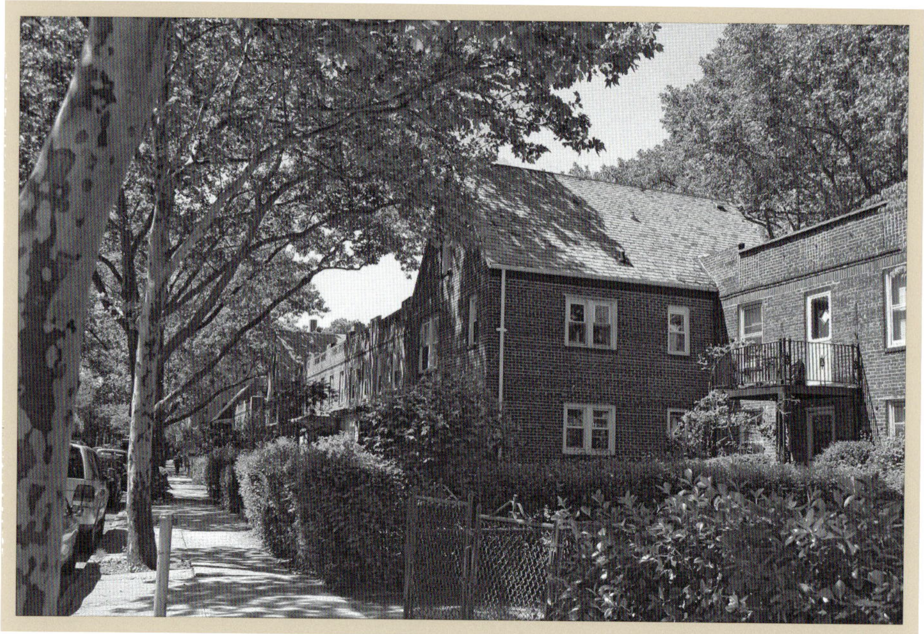

Sunnyside Gardens, recently designated as a New York City Landmark District, was one of the nation's first planned communities. It features generous rear gardens and landscaped central courts. Automobiles were banned to garages at the edge of the community. Sunnyside Gardens Park is one of only two private parks in New York City. When first opened in 1926, so many young families flocked here from Greenwich Village that it was dubbed the "Nursery of Greenwich Village." (Then photograph courtesy the Sunnyside Foundation.)

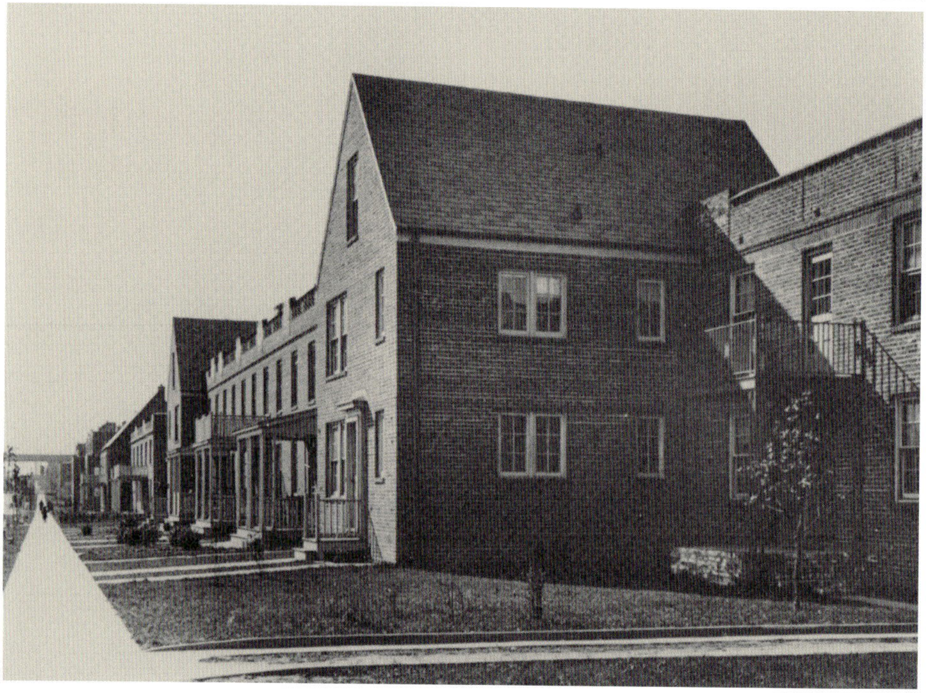

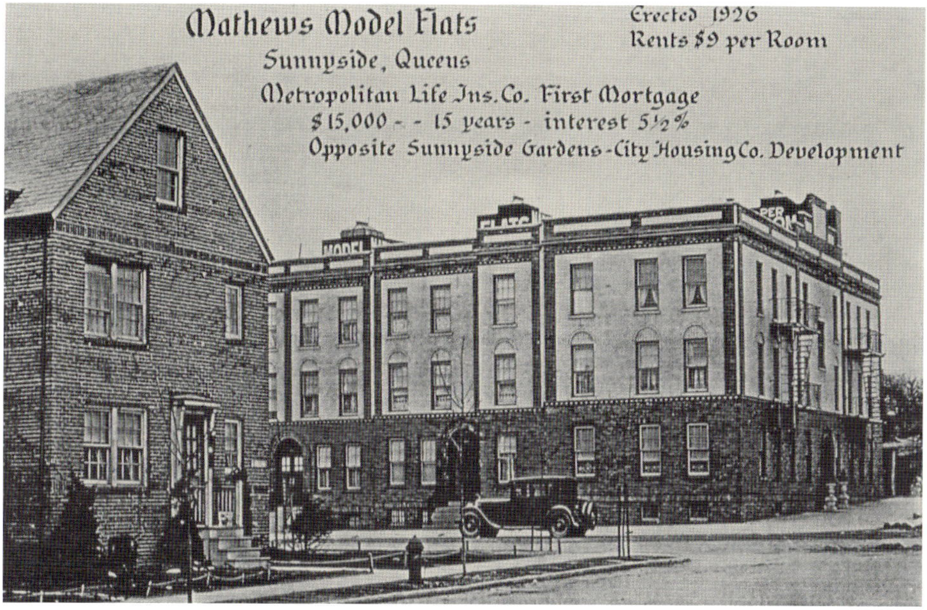

Two very interesting building styles are on 48th Street in Sunnyside. On the east side are Mathews Model Flats (New York City model housing that won national attention during the Panama–Pacific Exhibition in San Francisco in 1915), and facing them on the west side of the street are the incomparable Sunnyside Gardens. Queens has the largest housing stock of model apartments and planned communities in the country. (Then photograph courtesy the Mathews family.)

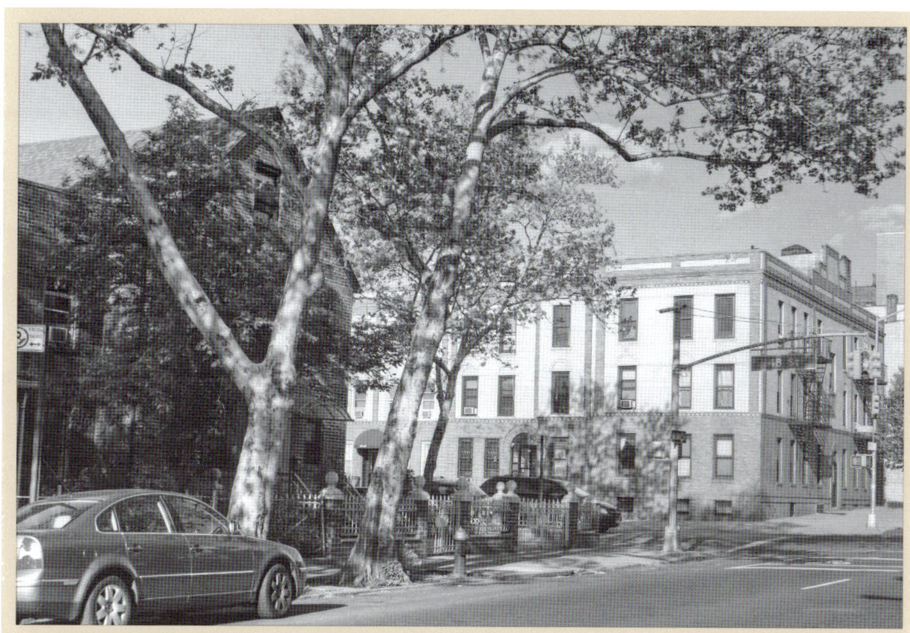

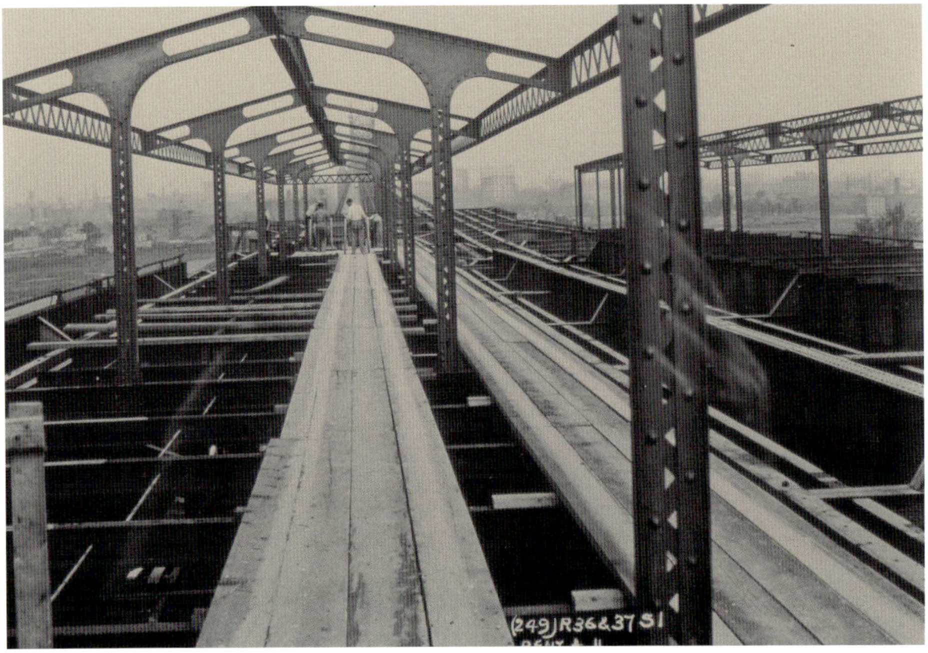

The Queens entrance to the Queensboro Bridge (1909) was graced with Bridge Plaza, a beautiful park around which streetcars looped and traffic split heading either towards Northern Boulevard or Jackson Avenue. Redubbed Queensboro Plaza when the elevated station opened (1916), the stop was to be the hub for an elevated transit network that connected Brooklyn, Flushing, and New York. It had two platforms on two levels, making it one of the transit system's busiest stations.

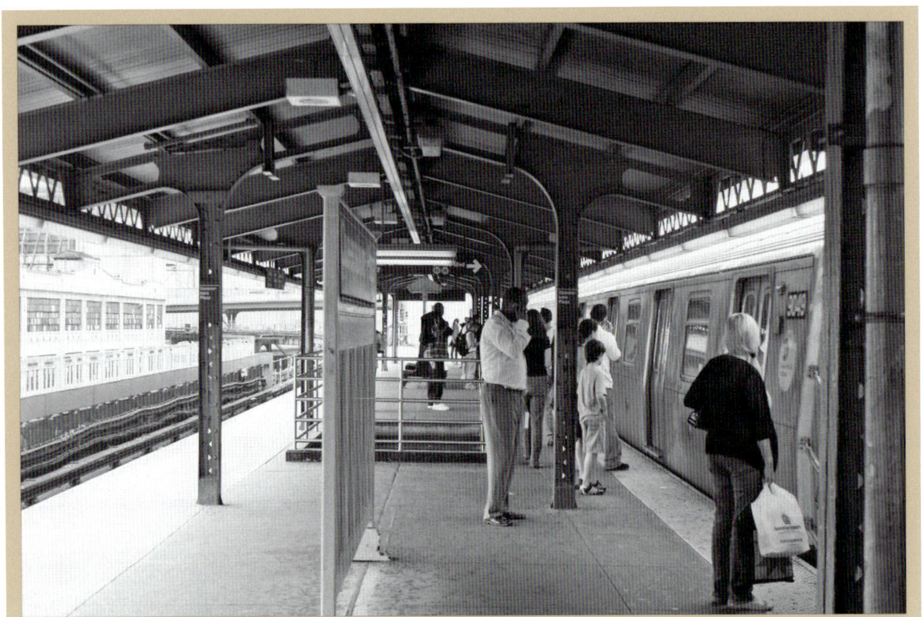

CHAPTER 2

Middle City

Dutch Kills, Ravenswood, and Astoria

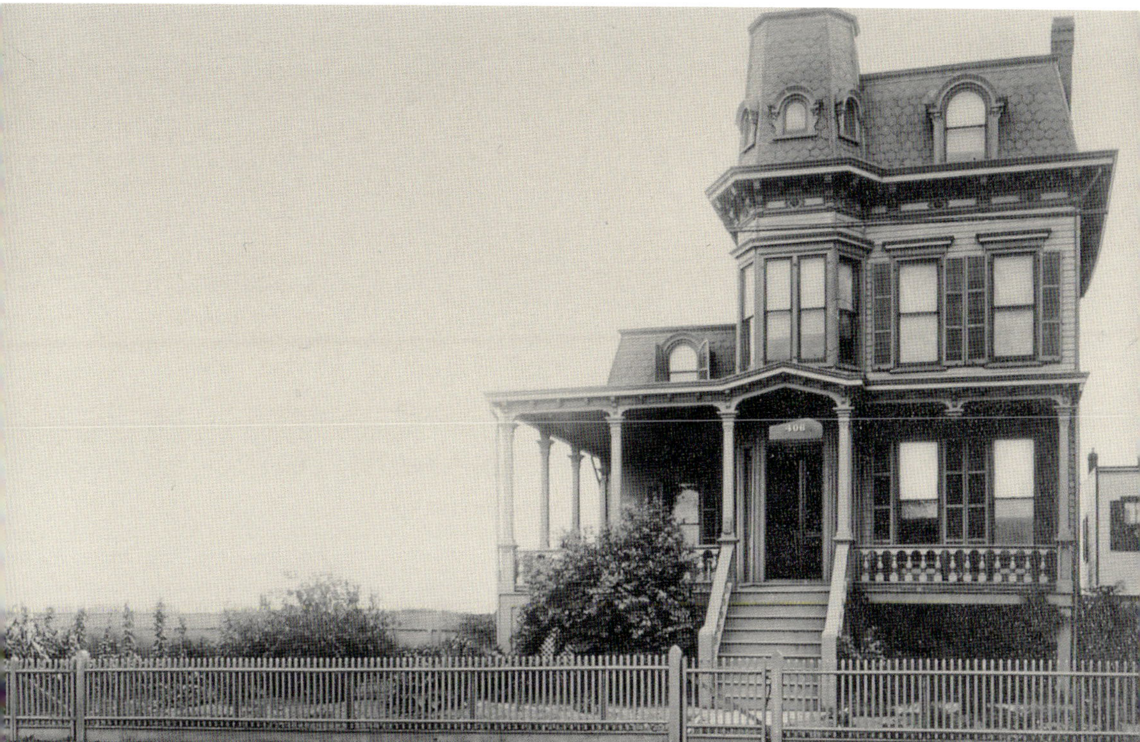

Prof. Ferdinand Quentin Dulcken was from a family noted as craftsmen of extraordinary harpsichords and as teachers of music to many of the crowned heads of Europe. A student of composer Felix Mendelssohn and friend of poet Henry Wadsworth Longfellow, Dulcken taught at musical conservatories around the world. The accomplished composer, pianist, and teacher came to America in 1876 and worked at Steinway Hall with members of the elite Steinway Artists. His house stands at 31st Avenue near 31st Street.

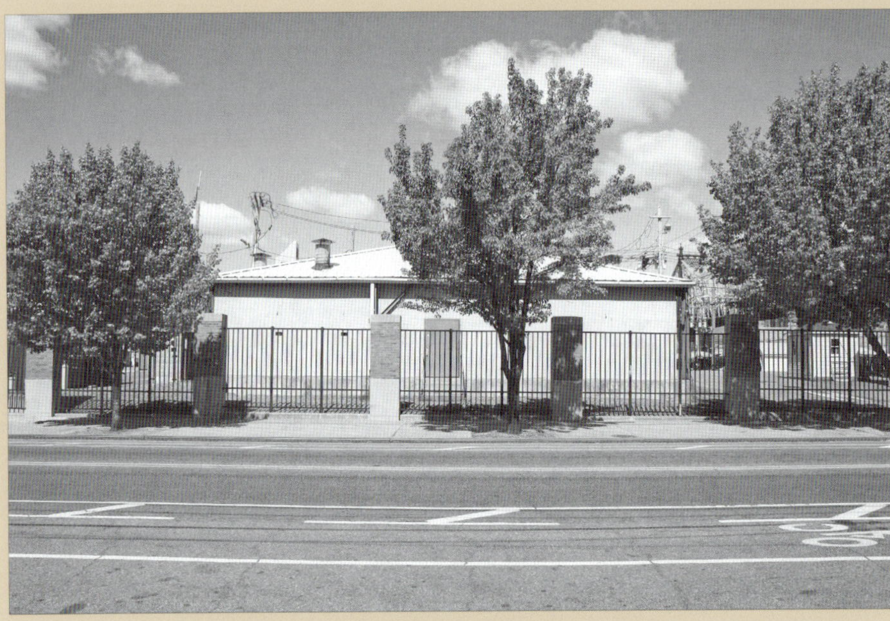

Bodine Castle, at 43–16 Vernon Avenue, was built in 1853 for John Bodine (1818–1887), a merchant who made a fortune in the Cuba trade. He ran an unsuccessful campaign for mayor of New York City in 1876. After his death, the building was used as an office for various businesses until Con Ed bought it in 1962. The Landmarks Preservation Commission considered it for landmark designation. The utility company demolished the last of the old Ravenswood mansions in 1966.

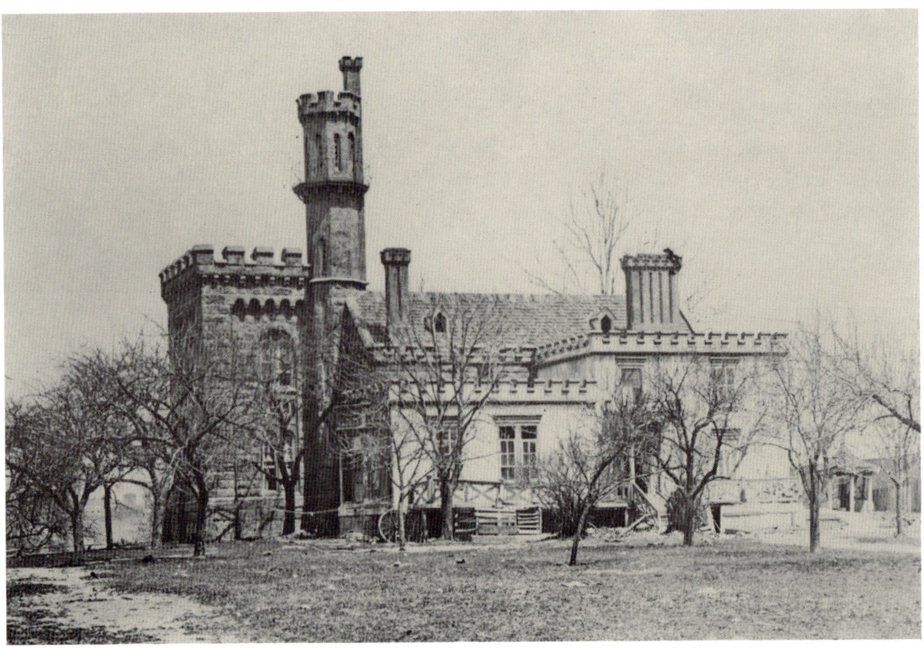

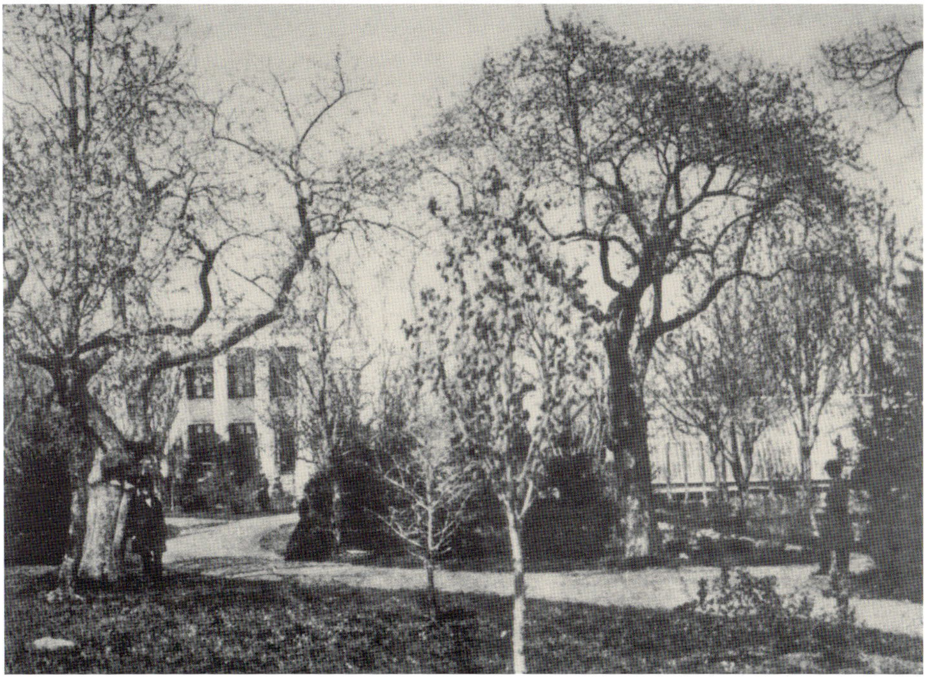

Pliny Freeman (1797–1879) amassed a fortune in the dry goods business. He became interested in life insurance and was the first president of the New York Life Insurance Company (1854) before resigning to found the Globe Mutual Life Insurance Company a decade later. Freeman financed the Vernon Avenue streetcar line in 1874. The mansion, greenhouses, and trees are gone; only the wall near 35th Avenue on Vernon Boulevard remains. (Then photograph courtesy Vincent Seyfried.)

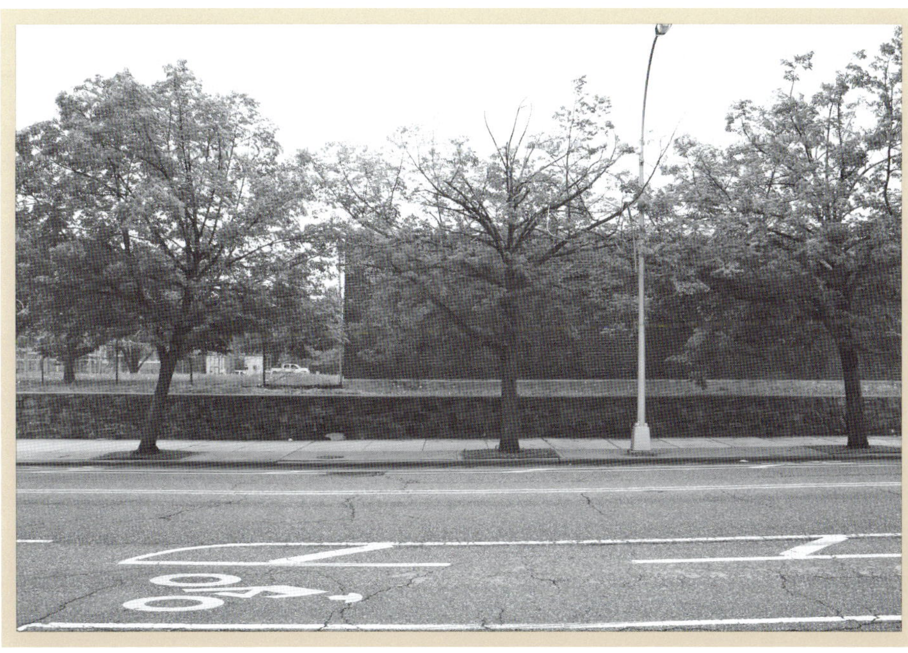

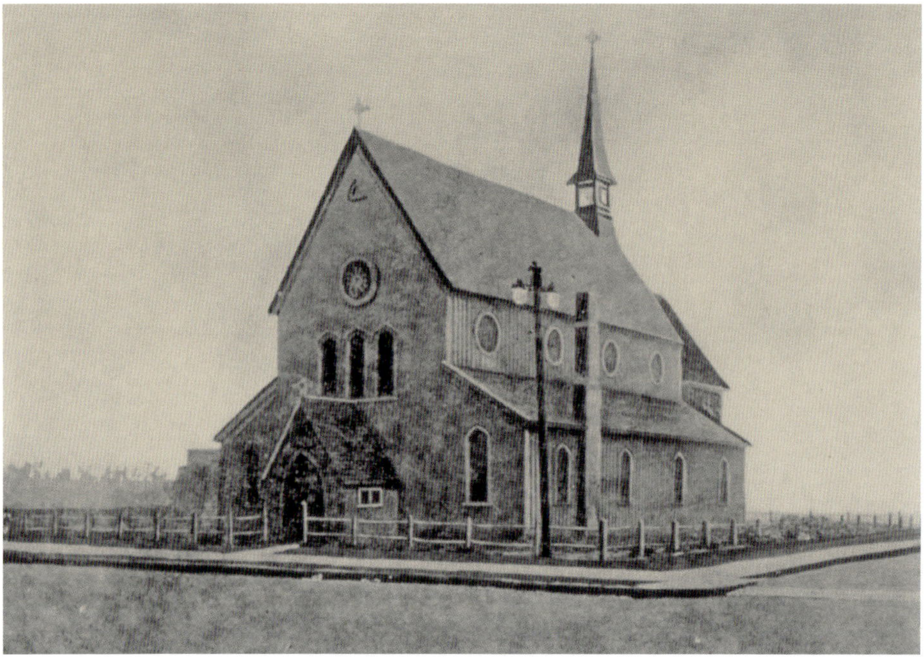

St. Thomas Protestant Episcopal, organized in 1849, was at 38th Avenue and Vernon Boulevard. Its reign as the fashionable church for the wealthy who lived in their Ravenswood mansions was brief. After 1875, the area quickly became commercial, as big plots of East River waterfront property were ideally suited for warehouses and factories. The church lost its congregation and was unable to support a minister. Services became intermittent, but the church did limp along until succumbing to fire in 1922.

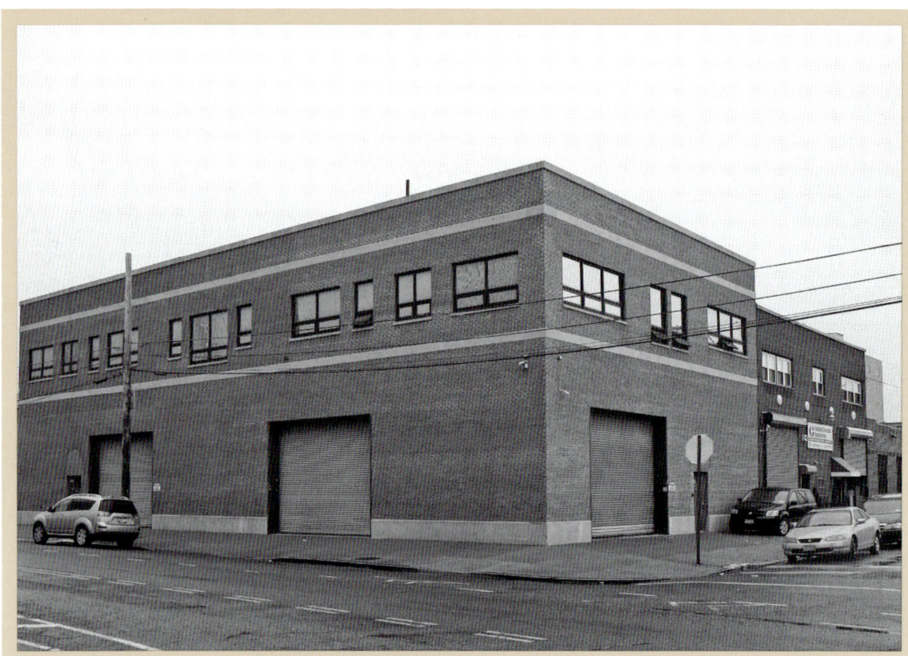

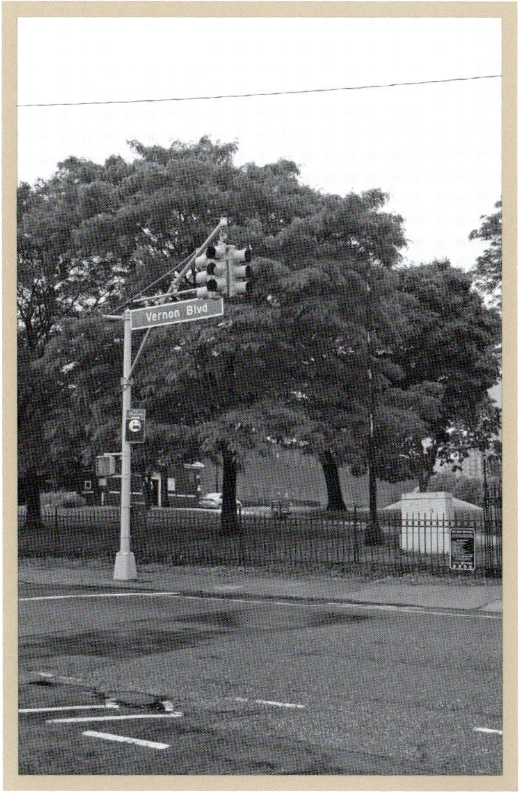

T. J. West (1859) and A. F. Smith (1873) were owners of this stately mansion. The city began to acquire property at the foot of 34th Avenue on the East River for a proposed Queensboro Bridge. After the project was moved south, the city named its Ravenswood purchase Rainey Park in honor of the man who had worked tirelessly for over 30 years to get the Queensboro Bridge built. The mansion was gone by 1919.

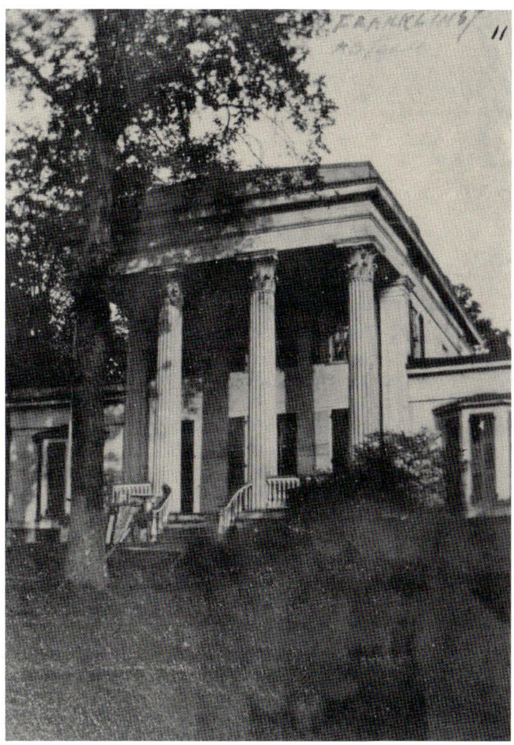

The Long Island City Fire Department became professional in the early 1890s. It purchased new equipment and built new firehouses. The Hook and Ladder and Chemical Engine No. 1 was on the east side of Vernon Boulevard near 37th Avenue. The name was changed in 1895 to Engine Company No. 6 and later, after 1898, Engine Company No. 160. On January 1, 1913, it became Engine Company No. 260. Company quarters are at 11–15 37th Avenue today.

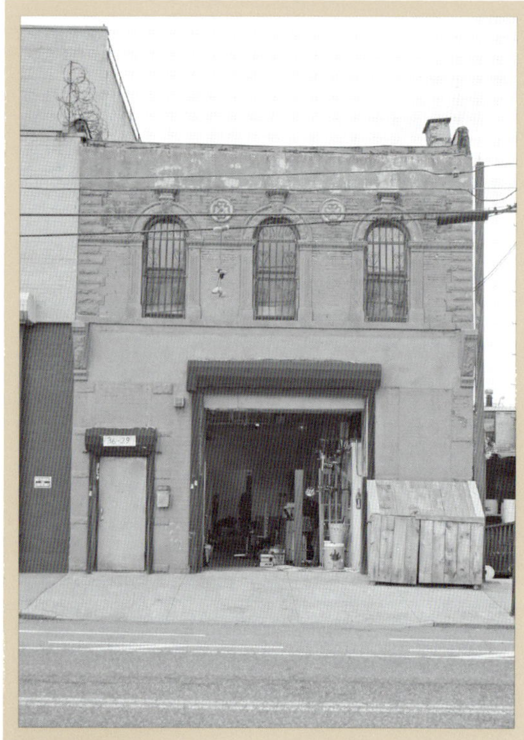

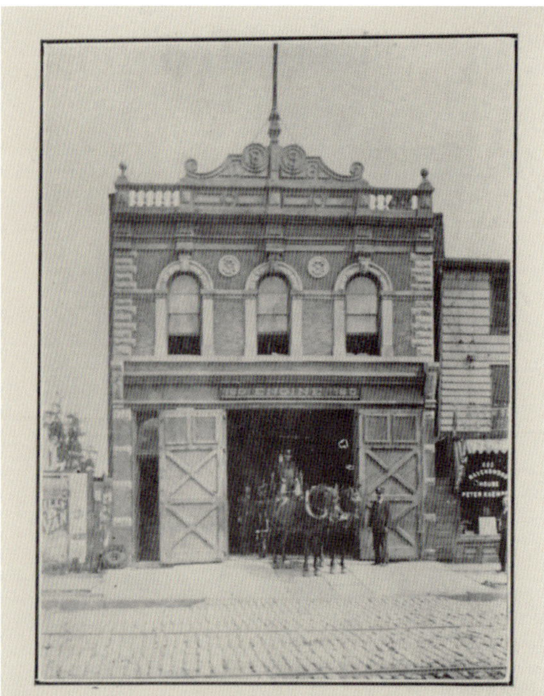

Engine Co. No. 160, Vernon Ave., Ravenswood, L. I. City.

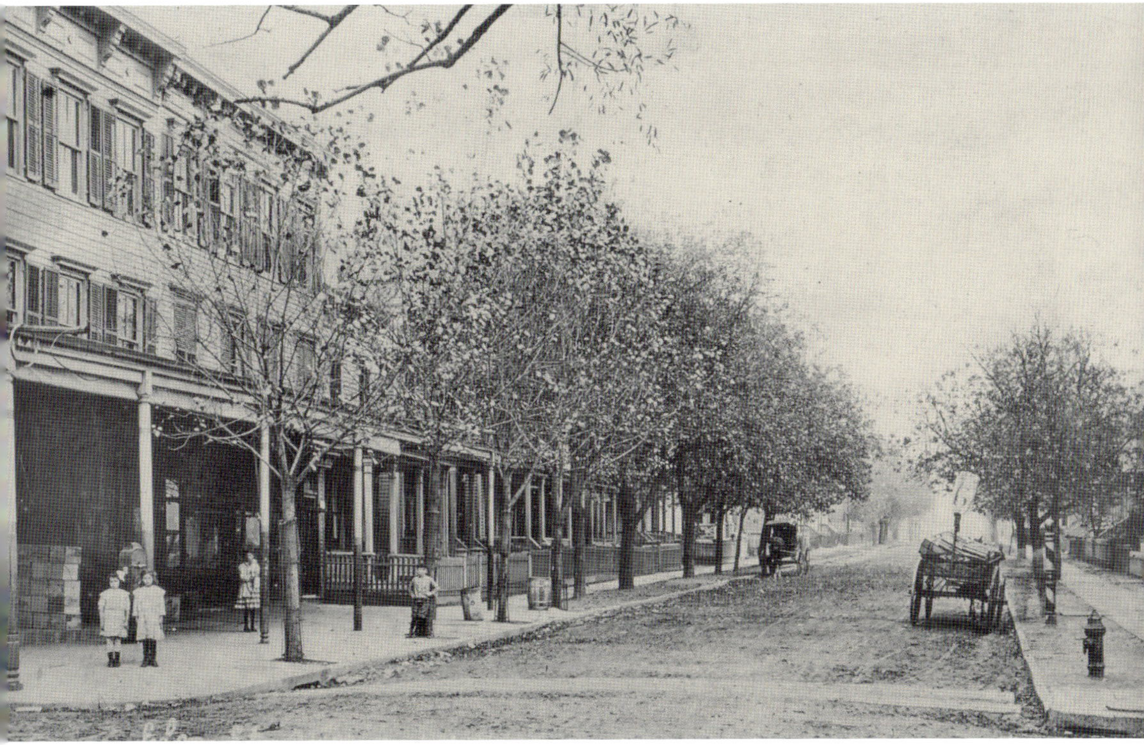

One hundred years ago, 30th Drive and 27th Street was an attractive residential section in Long Island City. The pleasant, neat appearance of the historic image stands in stark contrast to the modern picture. The sense of community is being lost as older buildings full of charm are being destroyed for denser development of prosaic design. (Then photograph courtesy Vincent Seyfried.)

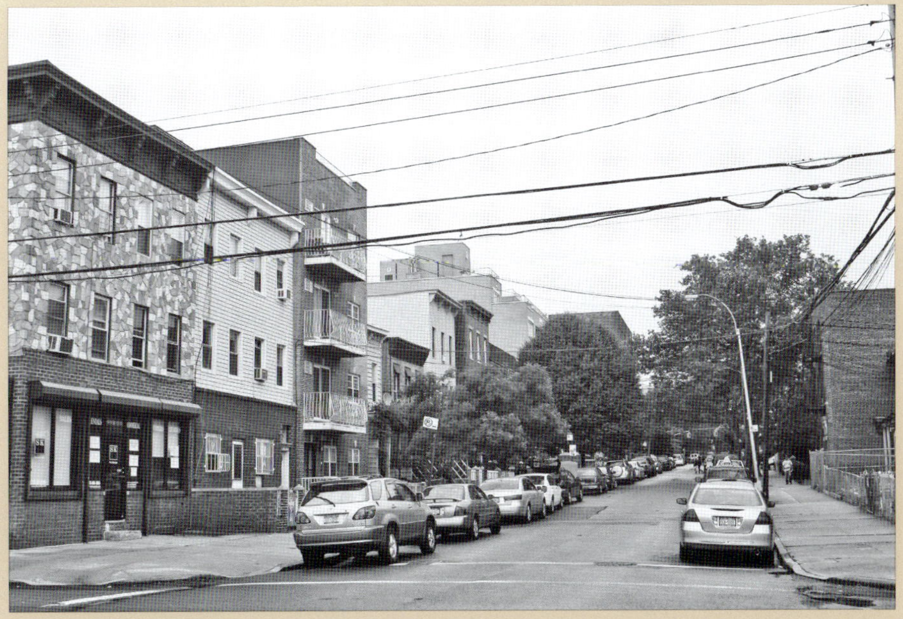

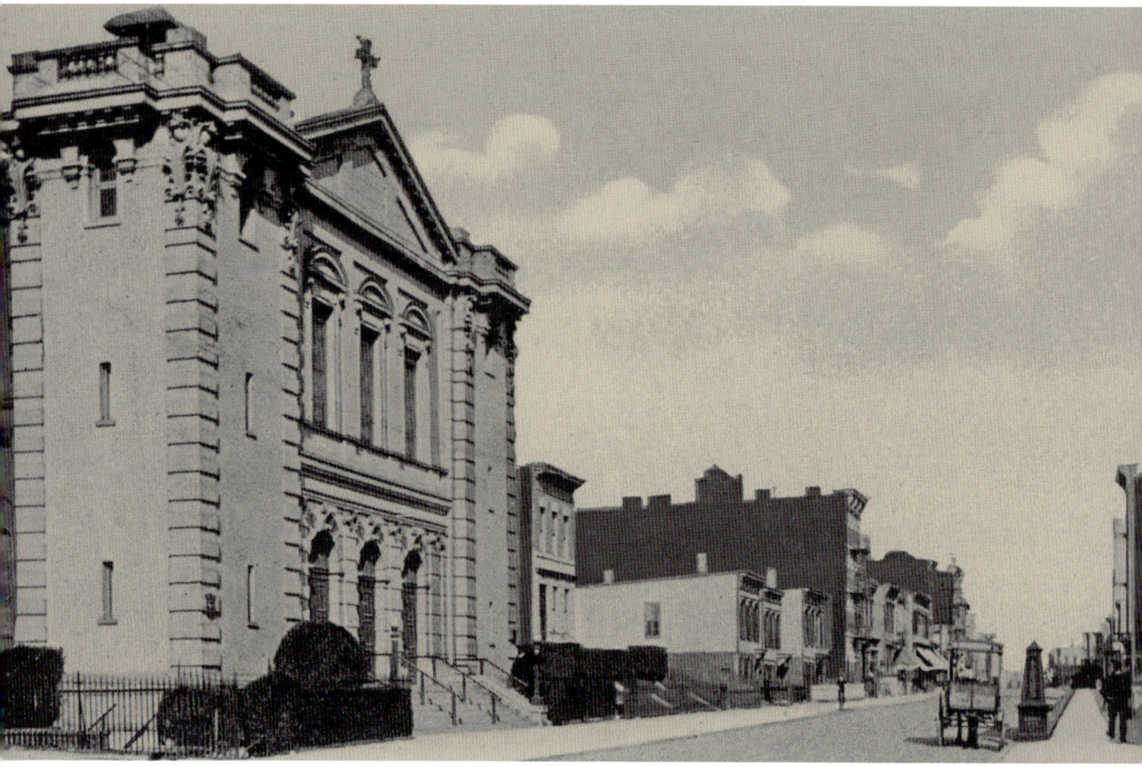

St. Patrick's Roman Catholic Church began holding services around 1869 for a small congregation. After growing out of their 1875 building, they built the current church in 1898 at the northwest corner of 29th Street and 40th Avenue. During the recent rezoning of Dutch Kills, a number of hotels were built in the formerly low-rise community; one is pictured on the right in the modern image. (Then photograph courtesy Gary Vollo.)

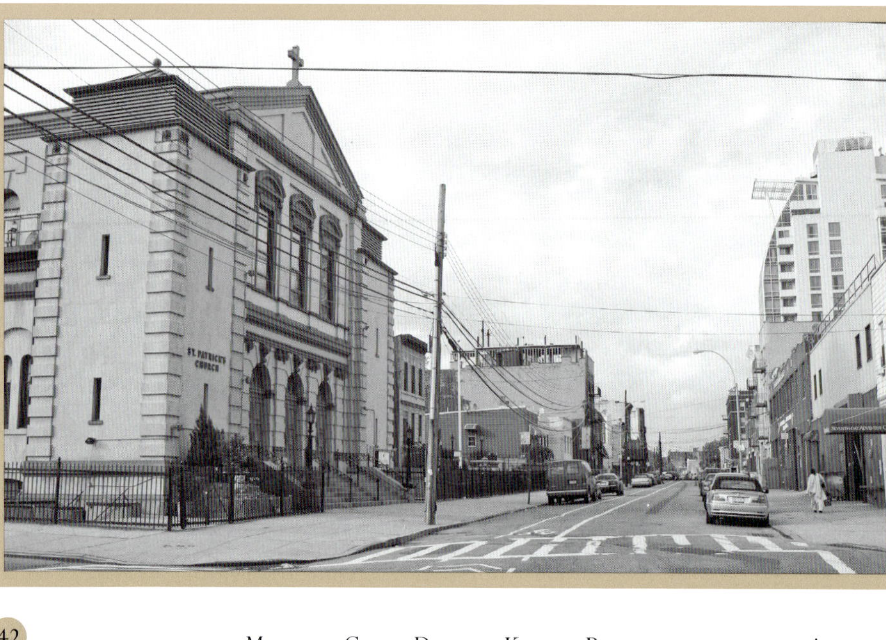

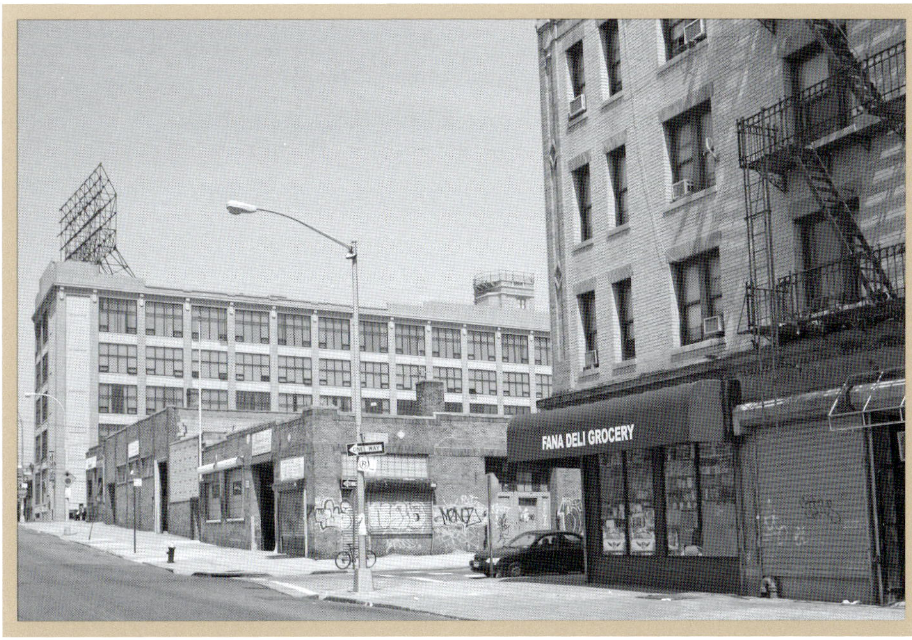

After the Queensboro Bridge opened and elevated trains whisked residents to Manhattan in a matter of minutes, development, even in areas that were off the beaten track, received a big boost. Swept away by the tide of apartment buildings and industrial lofts, most pockets of older homes were soon obliterated. A cluster of such doomed homes are nestled within newer construction on 37th Avenue. (Then photograph courtesy Gary Vollo.)

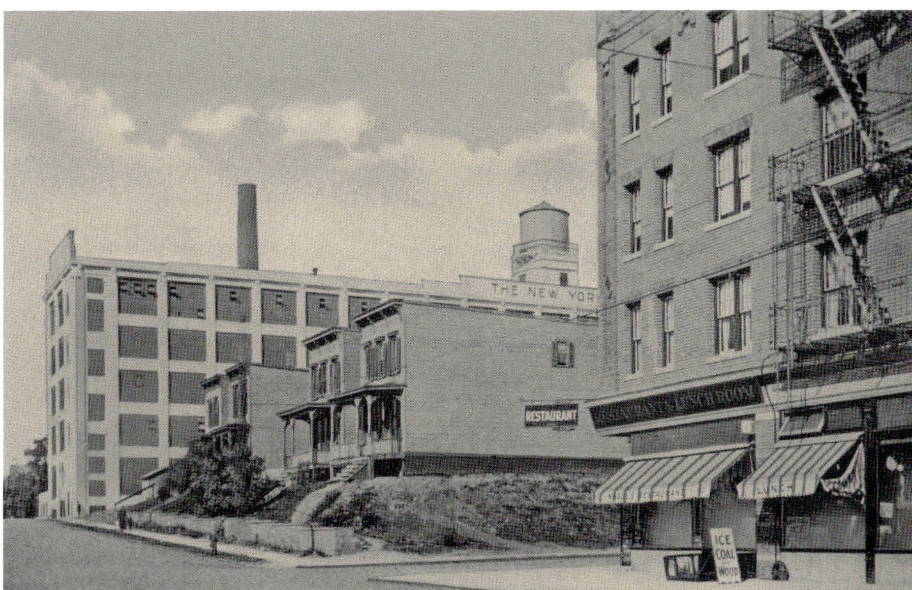

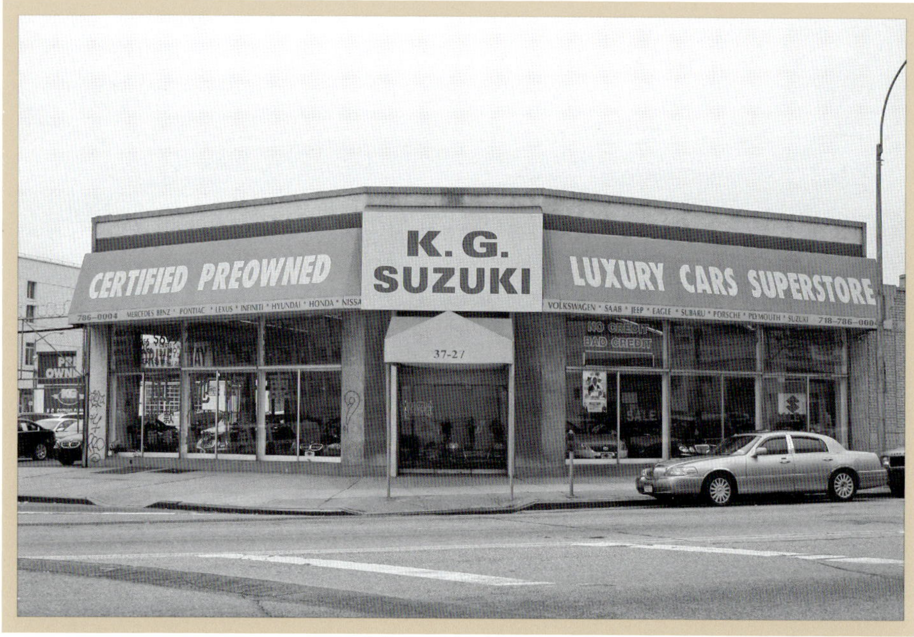

The Sunnyside Hotel, built by former circus performer Joseph Cook, once stood at the corner of 37th Avenue and Northern Boulevard. Around 1850, when steamboats stopped at the Ravenswood dock at the foot of 37th Avenue, the saloon quickly became popular with weekend crowds going to the Fashion Race Course in Corona. The picture was taken when the hotel was owned by Maria Nentwich some time after 1873. (Then photograph courtesy Sunnyside Chamber of Commerce.)

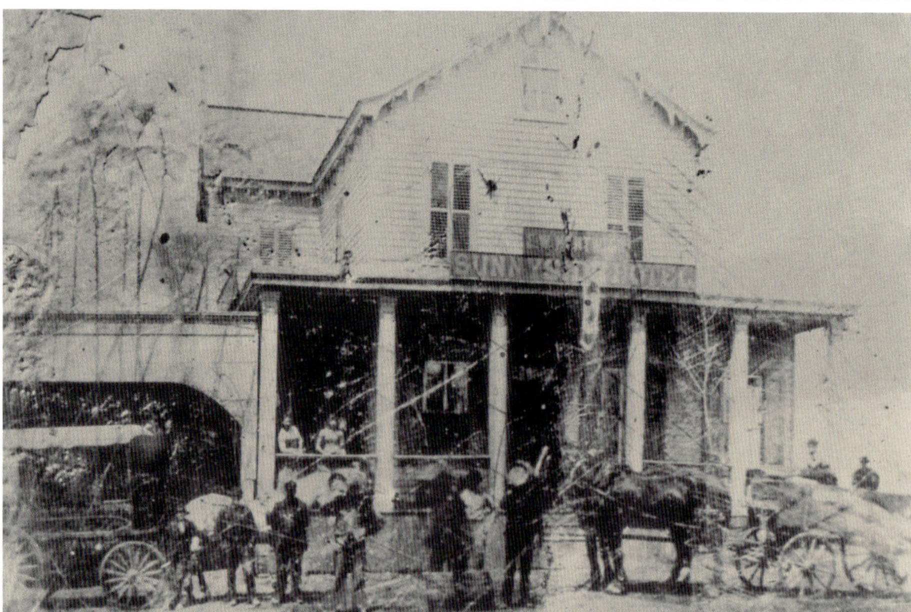

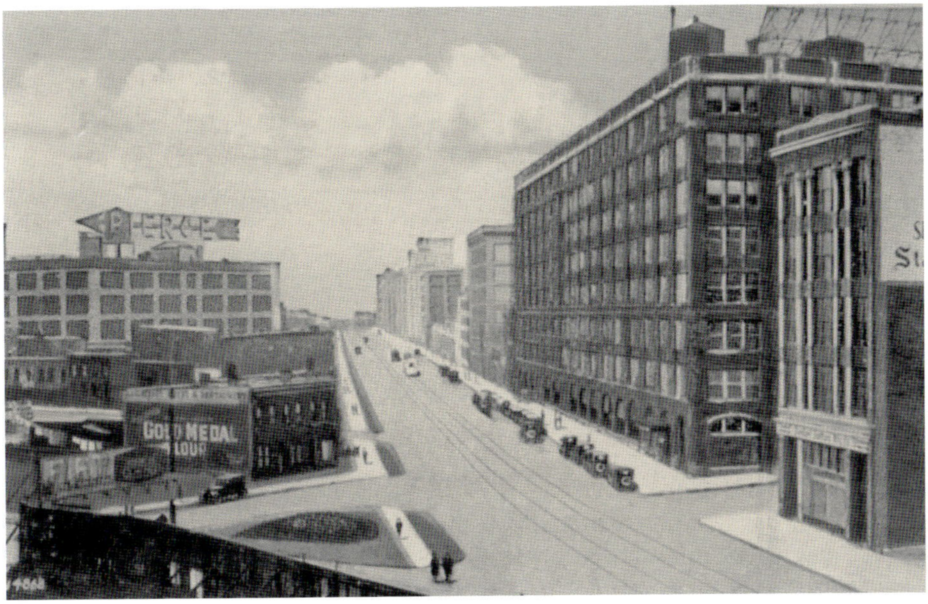

Northern Boulevard used to border a creek, Dutch Kills. The turns in the highway mirror the wandering course of the old marsh. The northern boundary of Sunnyside Yards is defined by a striking wall of loft buildings put up by Ford Motor Company, Ronzoni Pasta, Hellmann's Mayonnaise, and Karpen Furniture, among others. The building with the big arrow (left) advertising Pierce Arrow was a service facility for a now defunct automobile company. Some claim Henry Ford considered moving his production to Long Island City before settling on Detroit.

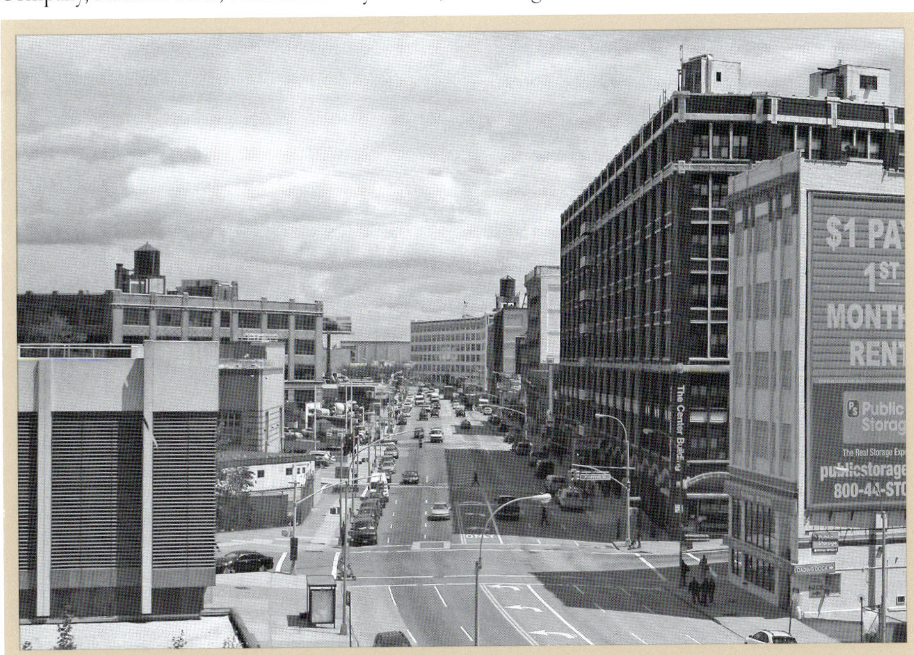

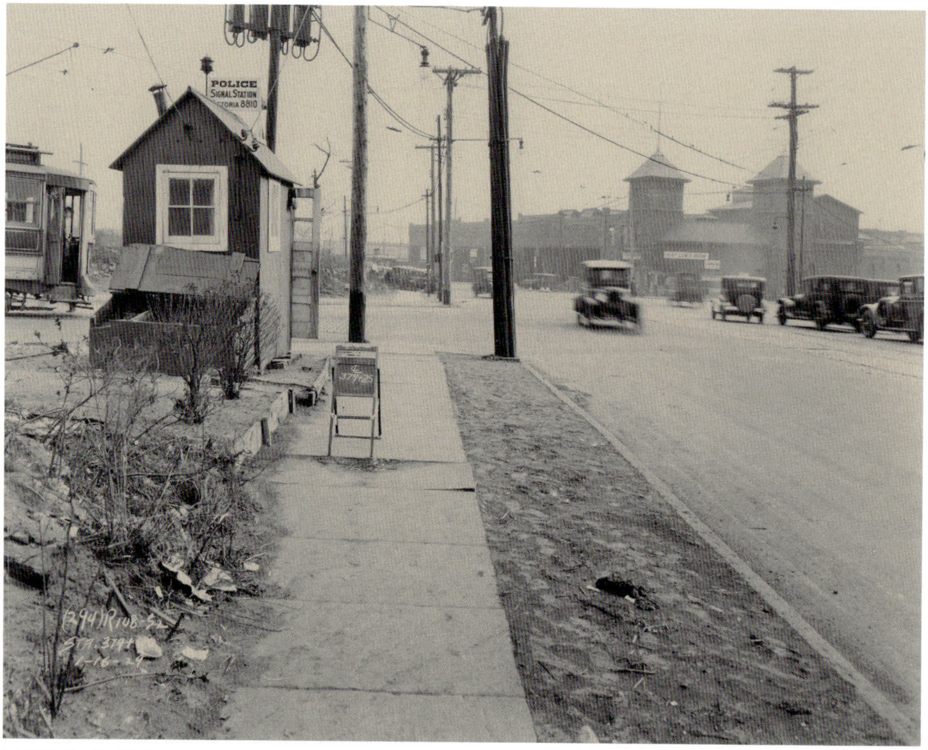

The Steinway Railway carbarns, built about 1895, were just over the city line at the southeast corner of Woodside Avenue and Northern Boulevard. The transit system was purchased by the New York and Queens Railroad Company, whose name is still etched in terra-cotta at the rear of the building. Only the waiting room (now leased as a pizza shop) and distinctive twin towers remain after demolition for a shopping center. (Then photograph courtesy Robert Singleton.)

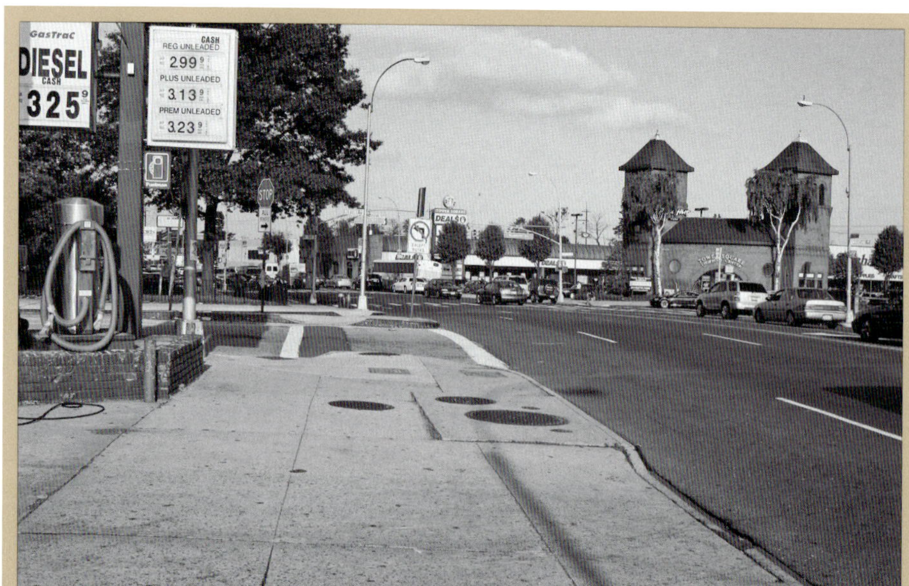

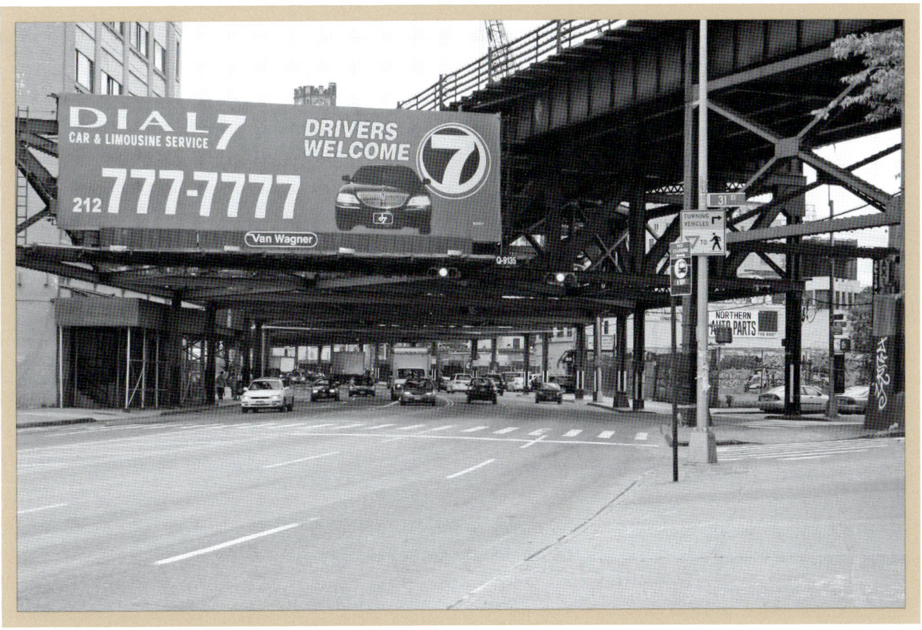

The topography around Queens Plaza underwent tremendous change when the Queensboro Bridge and Sunnyside Yards were built. Over 2 million cubic yards of earth were moved in the latter project alone. The busy streetcar line, shown at a street regrading at Northern Boulevard and 31st Street, was also disrupted. The house (left, background) was the Civic Club (torn down 1907), and in the distant right is Schwalenberg's Park, which later became Queensboro Arena (1911), an outdoor boxing venue.

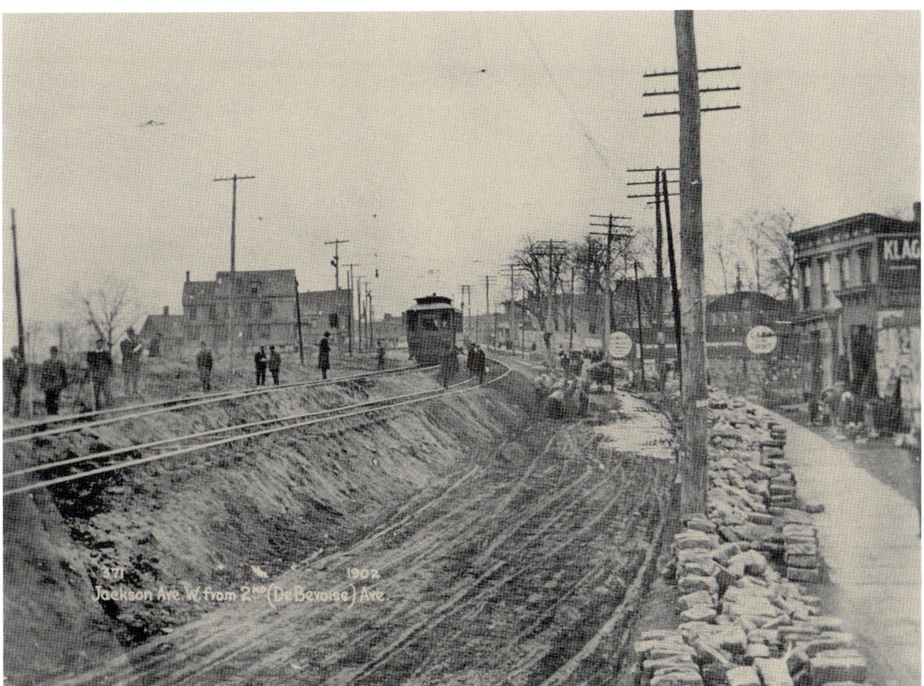

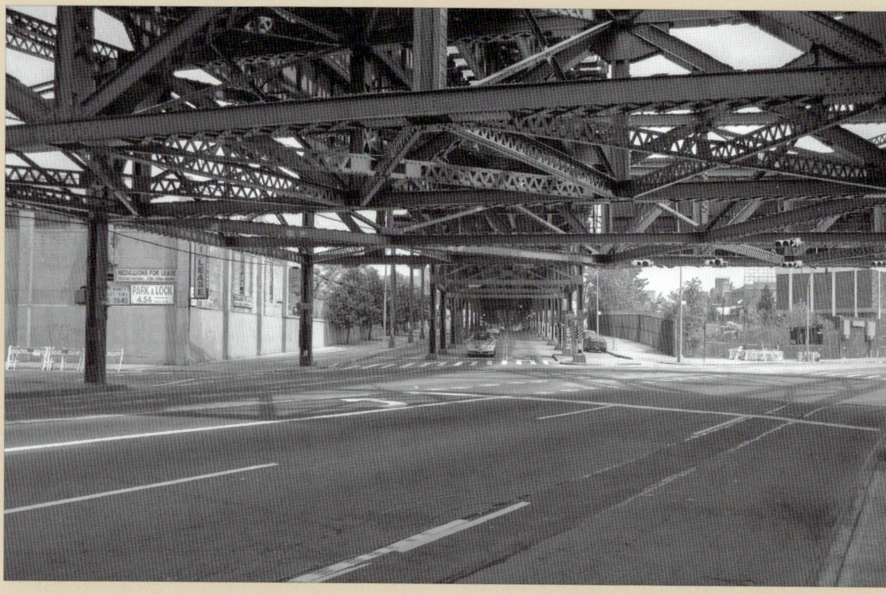

In anticipation of the elevated train, 2nd Avenue (today 31st Street) was widened some time after 1910. Note the streetcar tracks running up the middle of the road. This interesting view of Northern Boulevard and 31st Street would soon be filled with buildings in the shadow of a noisy, clattering elevated train. Service started between Queensboro Plaza and Ditmars Boulevard on February 1, 1917.

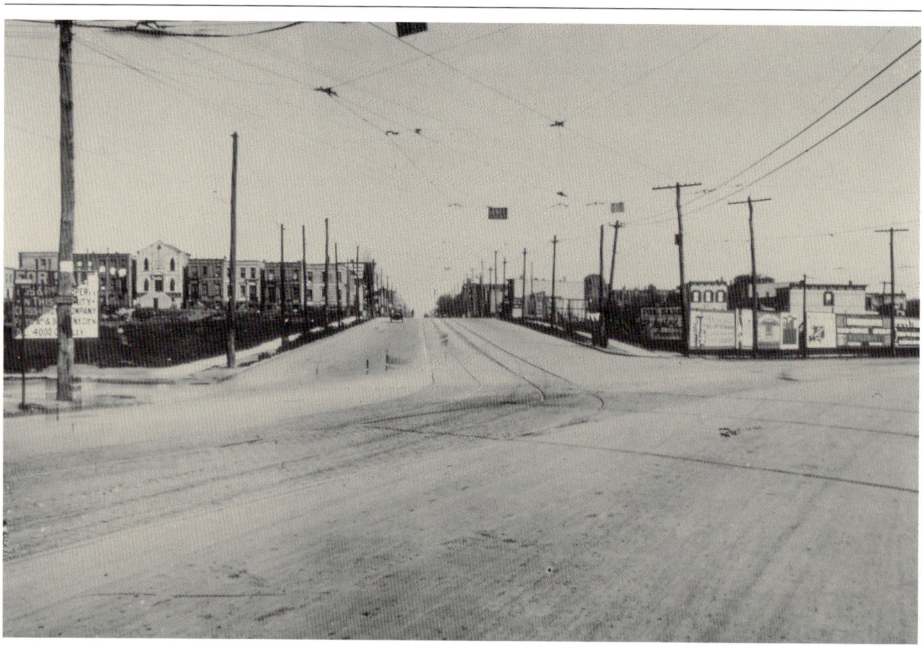

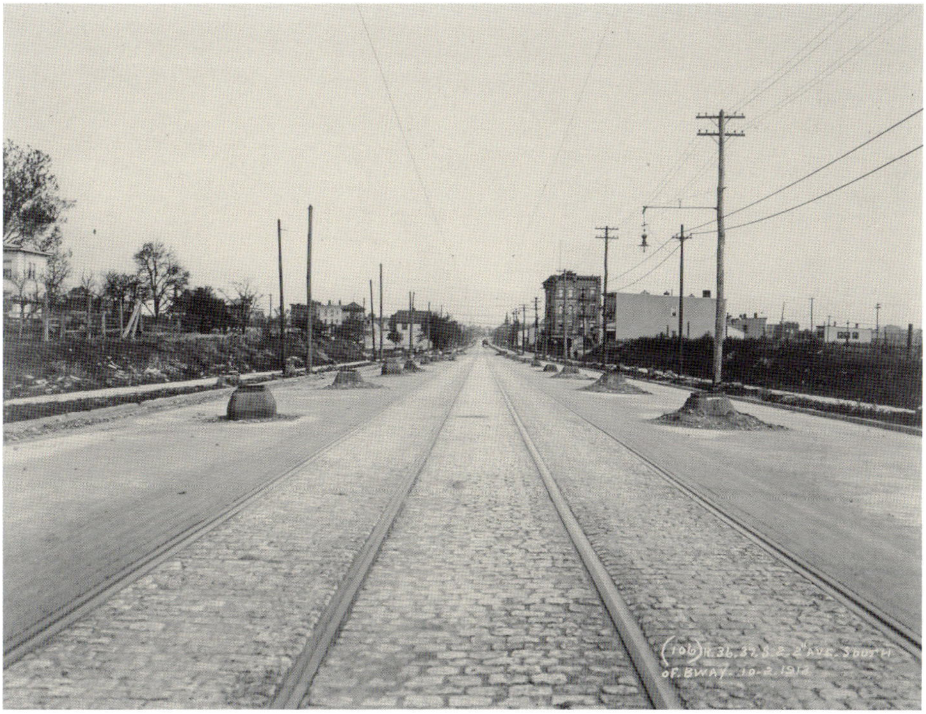

Rails for the Blue Line, trolleys connecting the 34th Street and 92nd Street ferries to Manhattan, once ran up the middle of 31st Street. Looking north in this view between 34th Avenue and Broadway, footings for the elevated pillars are already in place. Although the building in the distant right is still at the northeast corner of Broadway a century later, the open fields would soon be covered with buildings.

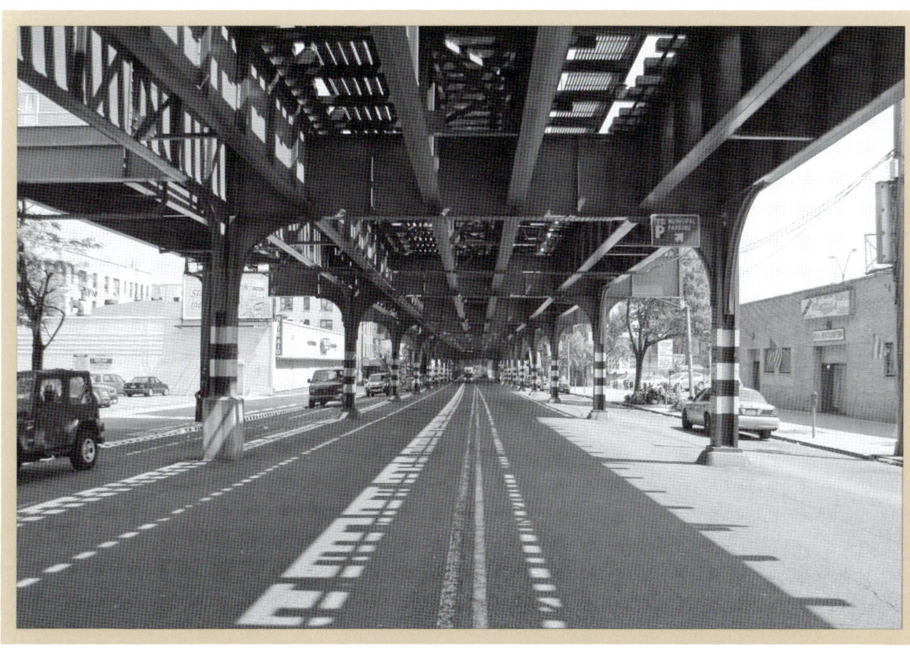

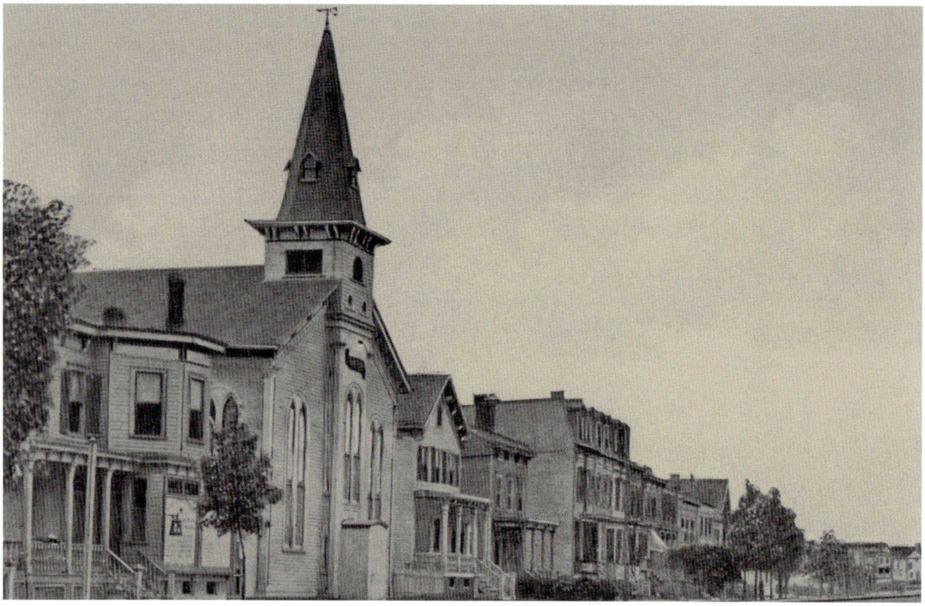

The Second German Reformed Church of Astoria was organized in 1855, and services were at first held in the Astoria Village courthouse on Broadway. A church, built in 1867 on 31st Street midway between 30th and 31st Avenues, was enlarged in 1889. Rev. Charles Steinfuhrer, pastor from 1867 to 1922, gave the benediction at the opening of the Queensboro Bridge in 1909. (Then photograph courtesy Gary Vollo.)

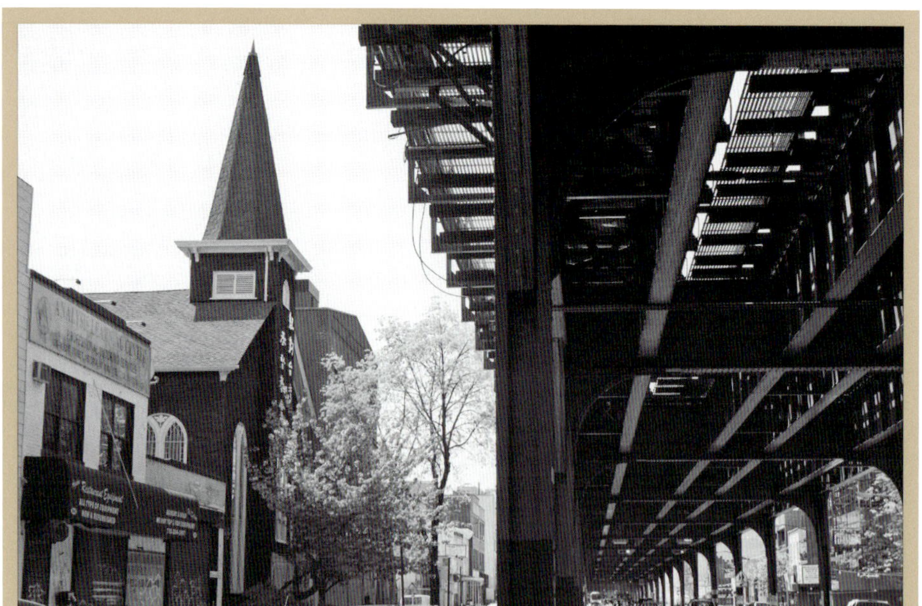

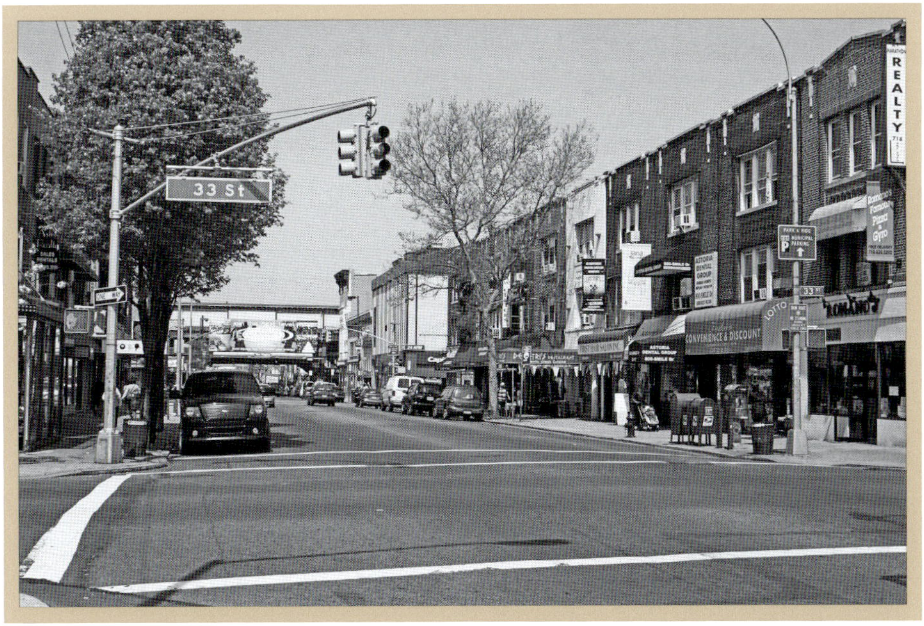

Horsecars were running to Schuetzen Park, at the corner of Broadway and Steinway Street, as early as 1875. Broadway was lined with mostly private homes and empty lots until the arrival of the elevated line. Seemingly overnight, property owners built a solid wall of buildings with street-level stores and apartments on upper stories. The stores with neat restrained signage made this an inviting shopping area. The Broadway Theater closed in 1961. (Then photograph courtesy Gary Vollo.)

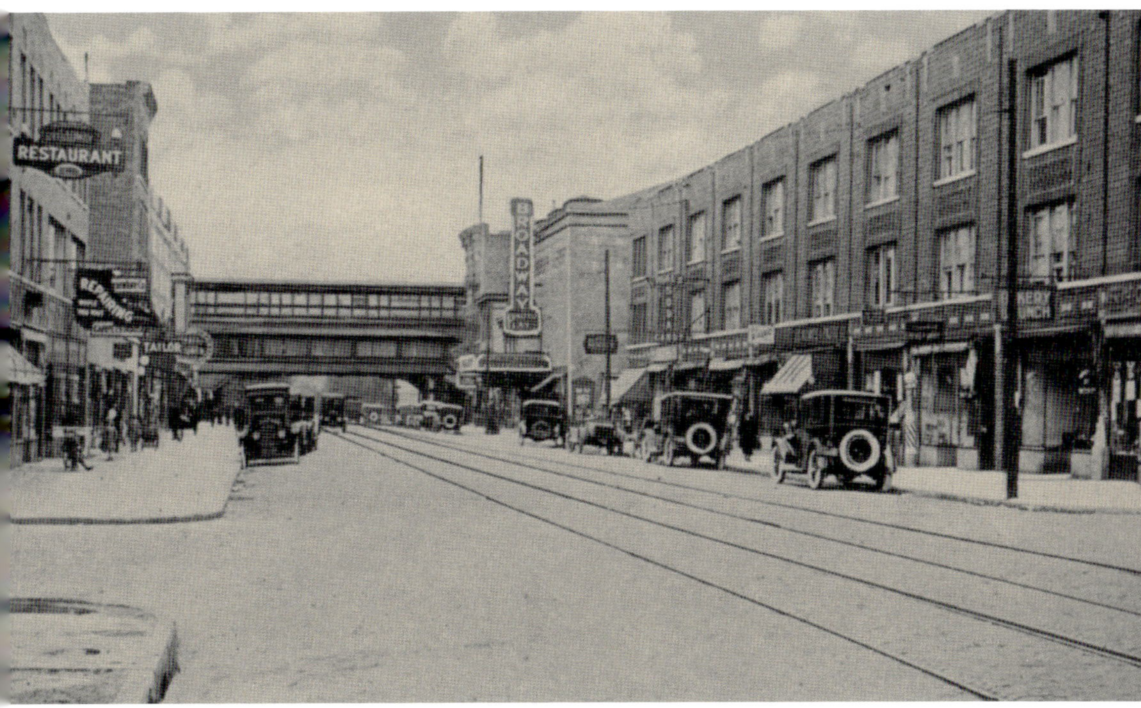

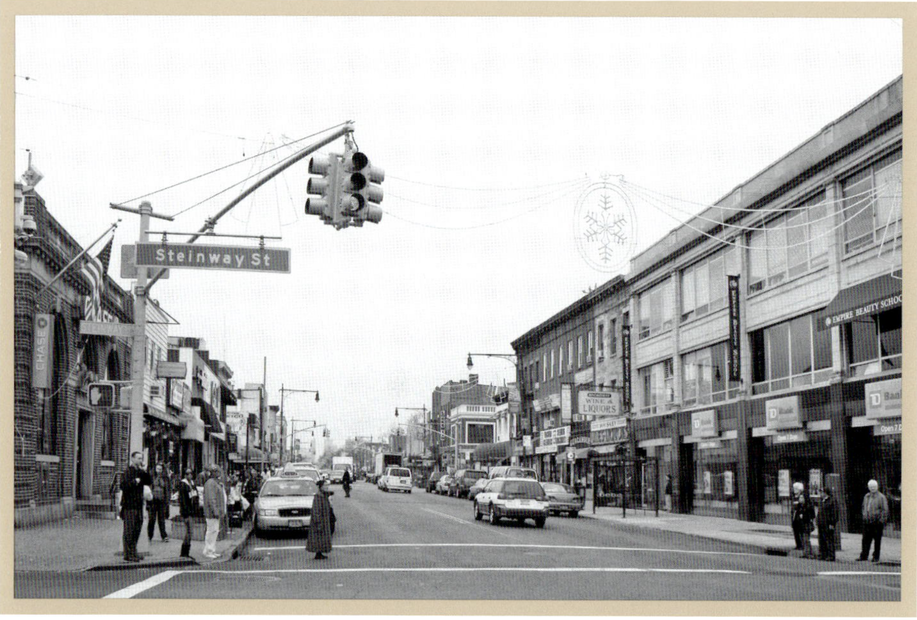

Steinway Street and Broadway has always been a key intersection, from the time when two streetcar lines met here to today, when the busy corner is served by several bus routes and the Steinway Street subway station. This view faces west down Broadway. Steinway Street and Broadway continue to be important shopping districts. (Then photograph courtesy Gary Vollo.)

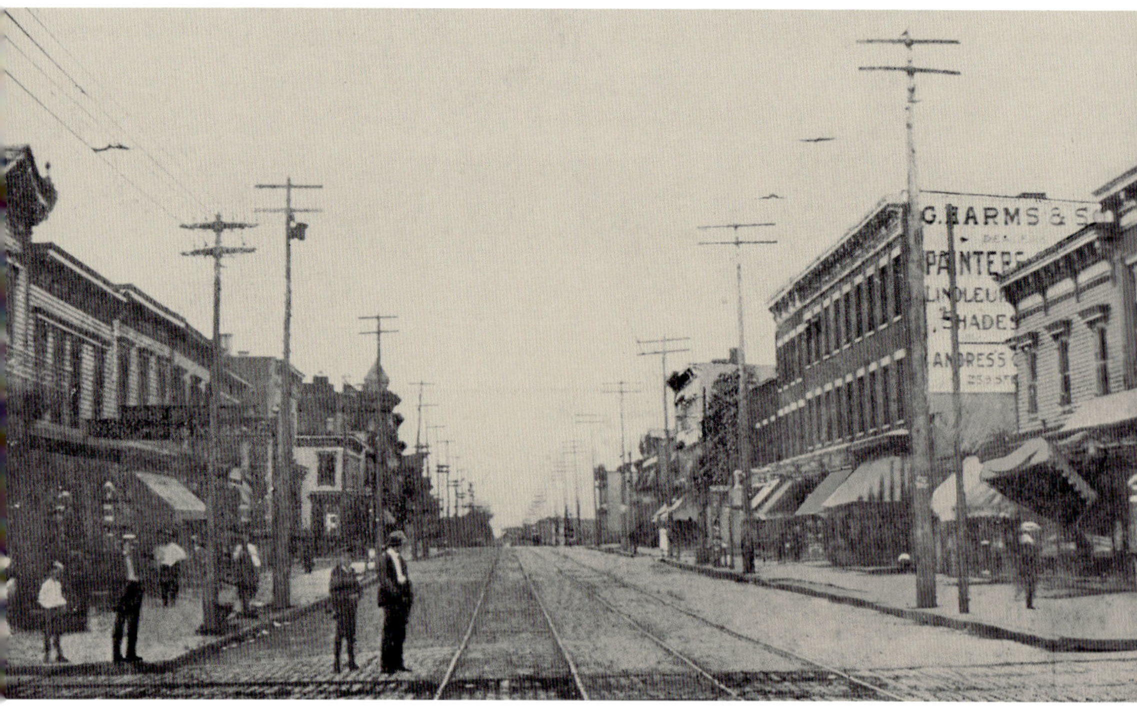

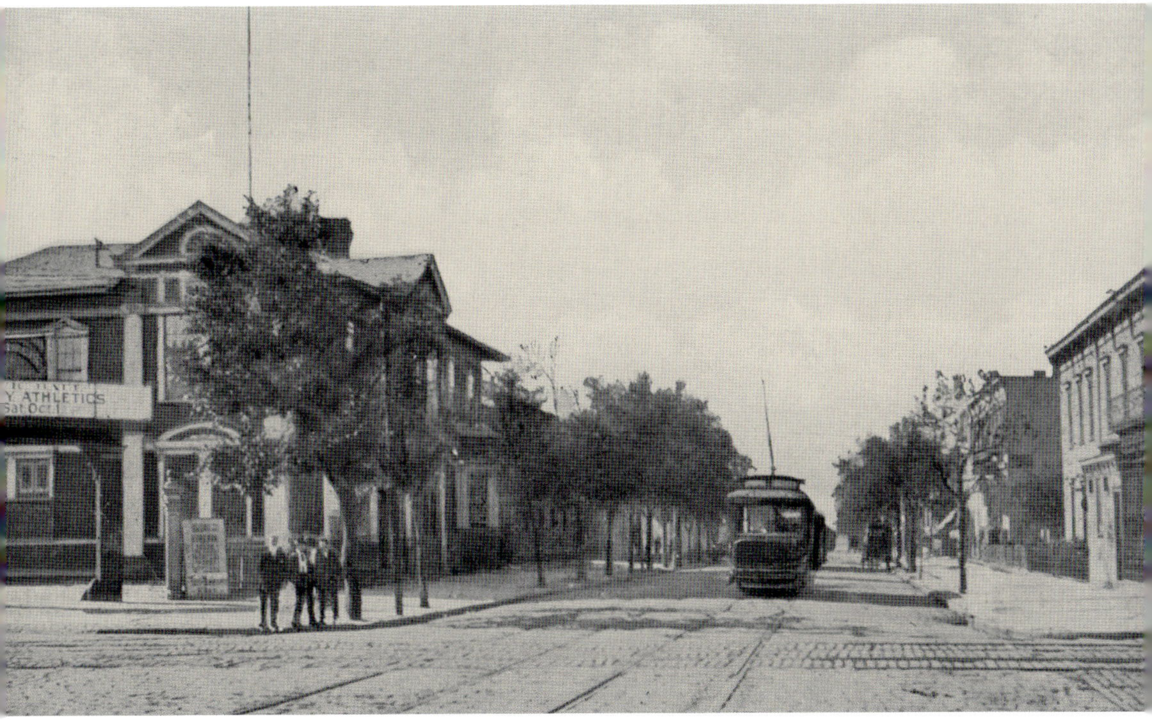

This is the same intersection of Steinway Street and Broadway, but this time with a south perspective looking down Steinway Street. To the left was Schuetzen Park, a beer garden and picnic ground that for more than 50 years was one of the leading political and social venues in the borough. It was patronized by everyone from presidents on the campaign trail to families out for a day. (Then photograph courtesy Gary Vollo.)

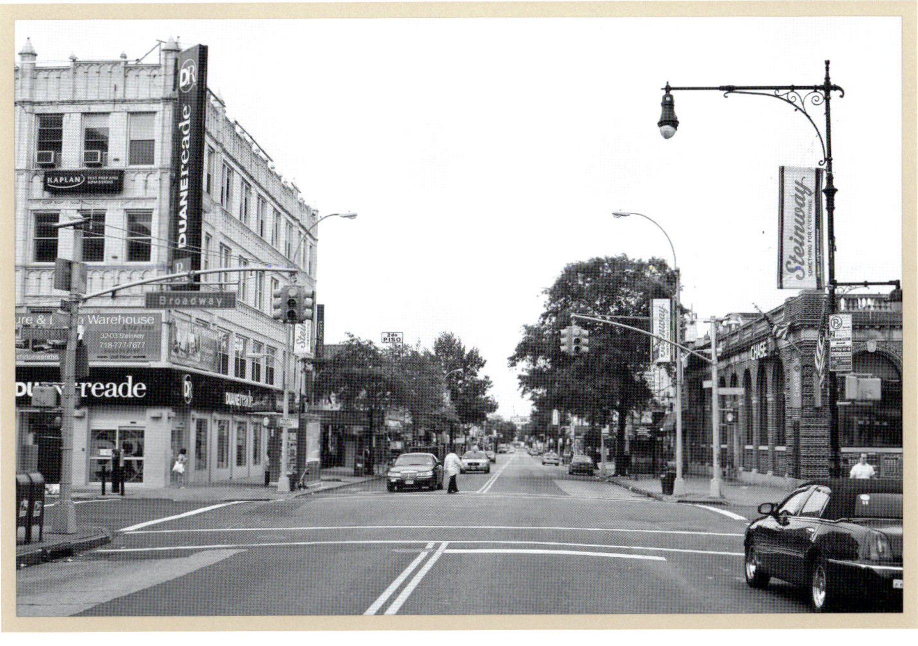

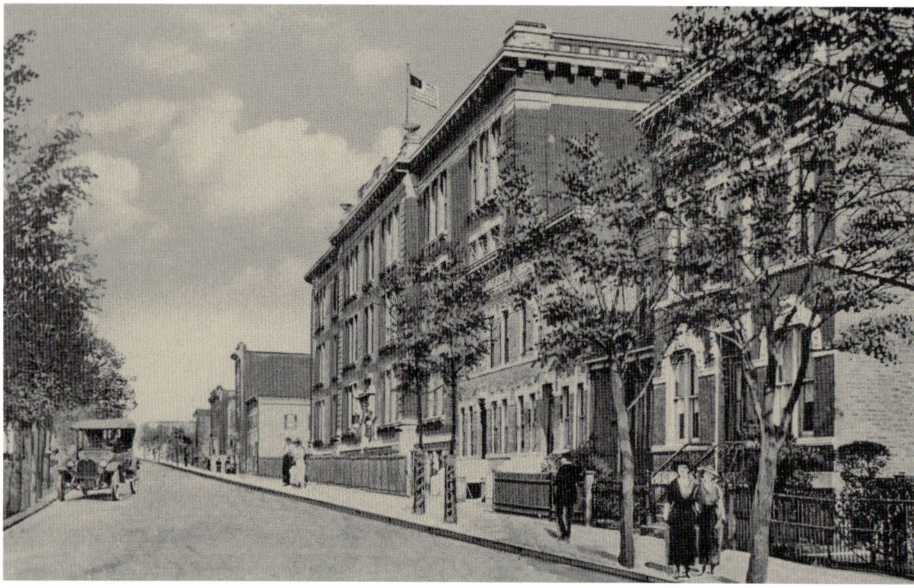

The cornerstone for the Fourth Ward Primary School was laid on Thanksgiving Day 1885. The school, usually called P.S. 6, stood on the east side of 38th Street between 31st Avenue and Broadway. It was enlarged in 1906 with an addition that extended through the block to Steinway Street. By the 1920s, it had more than 2,000 students and 50 teachers. The building was torn down and replaced with a playground and a parking lot. (Then photograph courtesy Gary Vollo.)

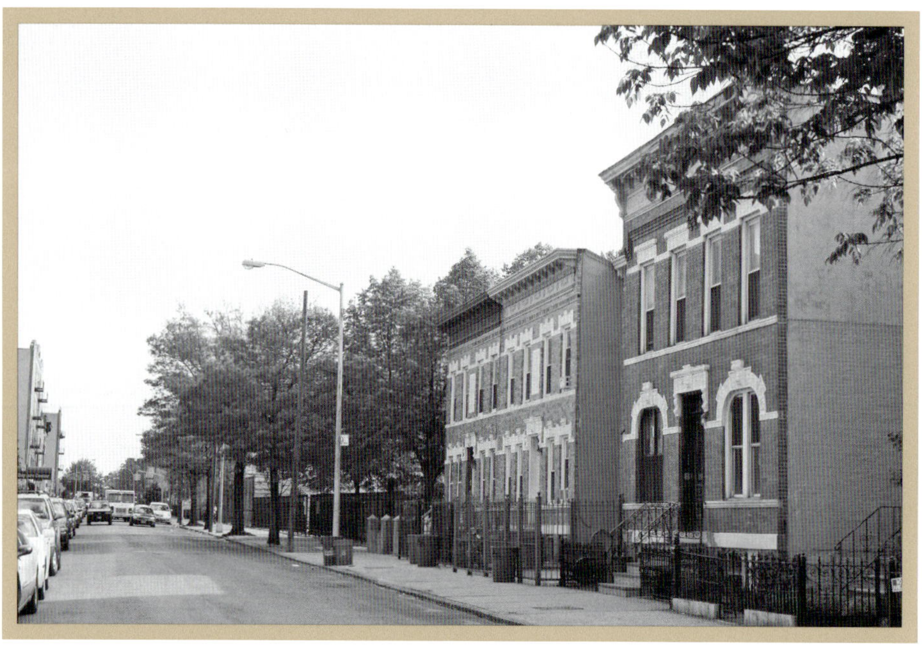

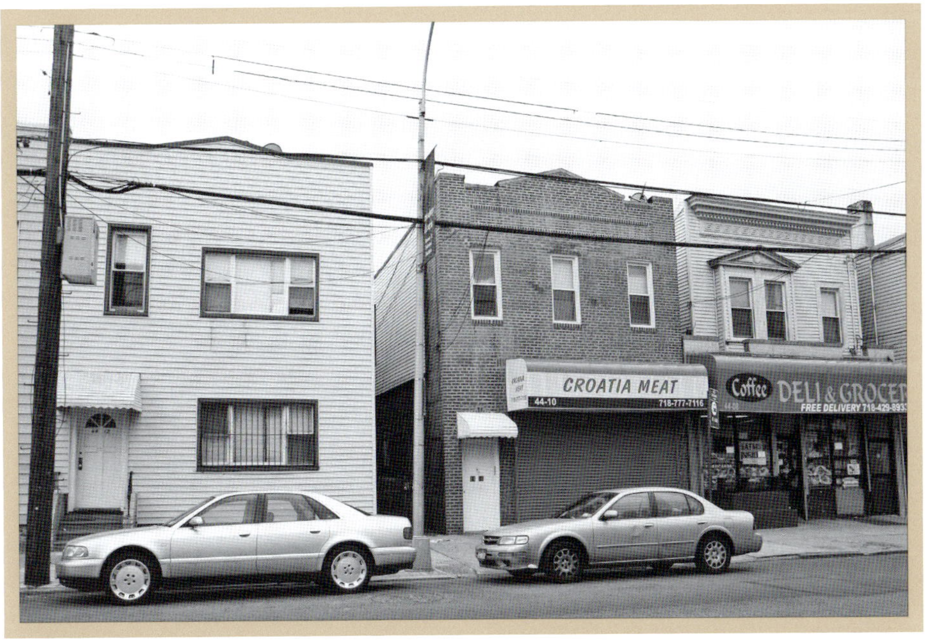

Buildings, even homes of modest means, were embellished with an attention to detail and quality of workmanship that is all but unheard of today. These were strong communities, since most residences were owner-occupied by people who had a long-term vested interest in the neighborhood. The upstairs apartment in the building to the right was used in the movie *Going in Style* (1979). (Then photograph courtesy Robert Singleton.)

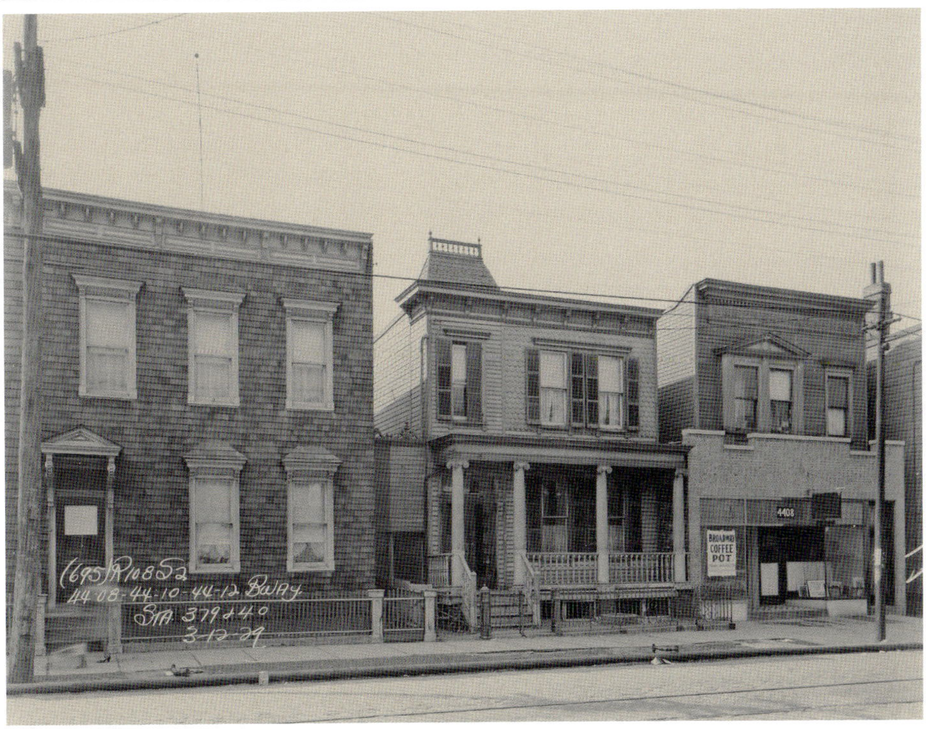

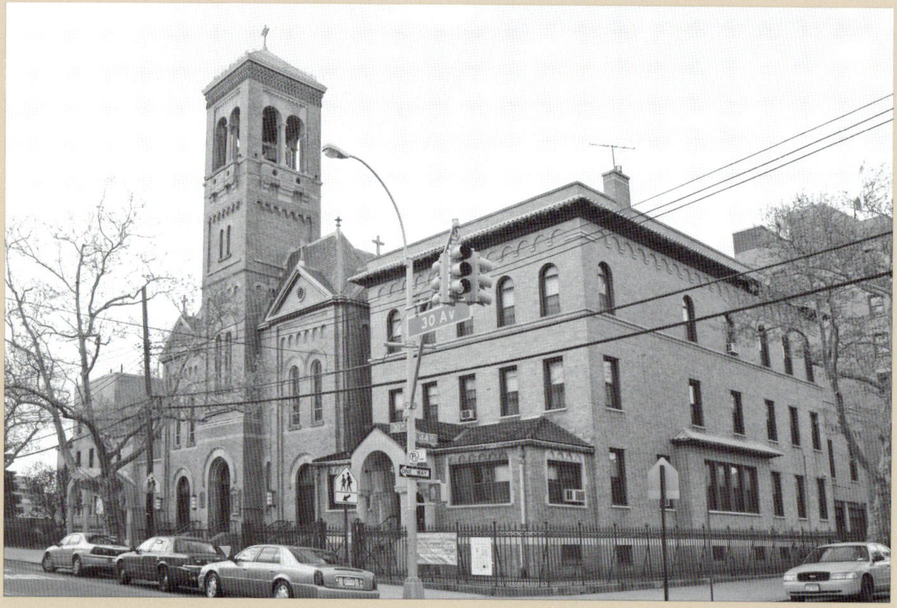

Blocks north and east of Broadway, purchased by members of the German Cabinet Makers Union, were called the German Settlement. The parish was organized in 1877 and dedicated to St. Joseph, the patron saint of carpenters. The current building, on the north side of 30th Avenue between 43rd and 44th Streets, replaced an earlier church in 1906. The complex was modernized a number of times with newer and larger facilities—a school (1918), a rectory (1928), and a convent (1937). (Then photograph courtesy Bob Stonehill.)

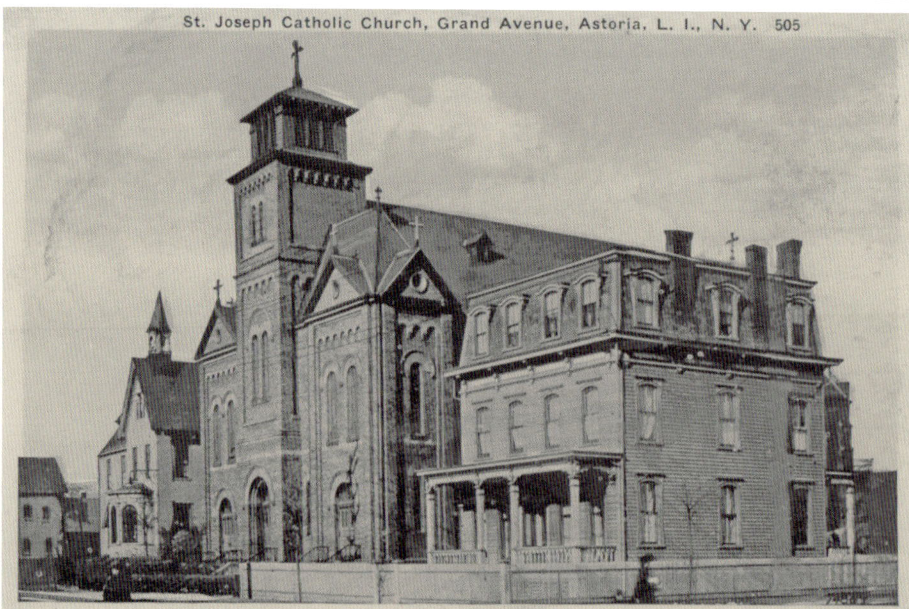

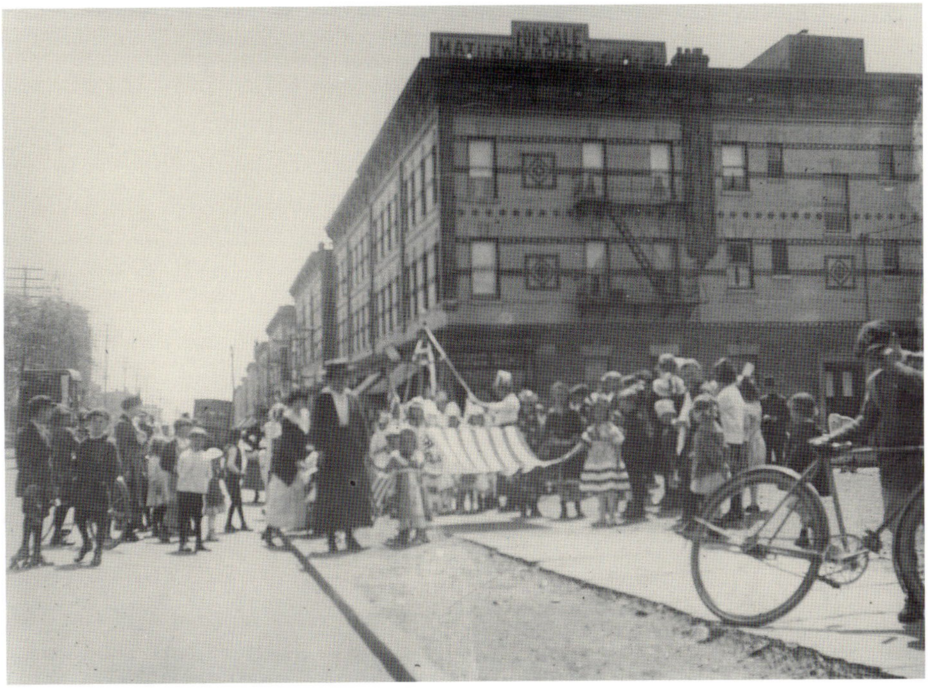

Starting in Ridgewood (1905), then Astoria (1915), Sunnyside (1920), and finally Elmhurst (1935), hundreds of Mathews Model Flats were built throughout Queens. Advertised under the banner, "Solving New York's Housing Problem," inexpensive, solidly built, and profitable to own, these legendary houses were reputed never to have suffered a foreclosure. G. X. Mathews was asked to build Stuyvesant Town in Manhattan, but he declined, believing he could not maintain quality on a large project.

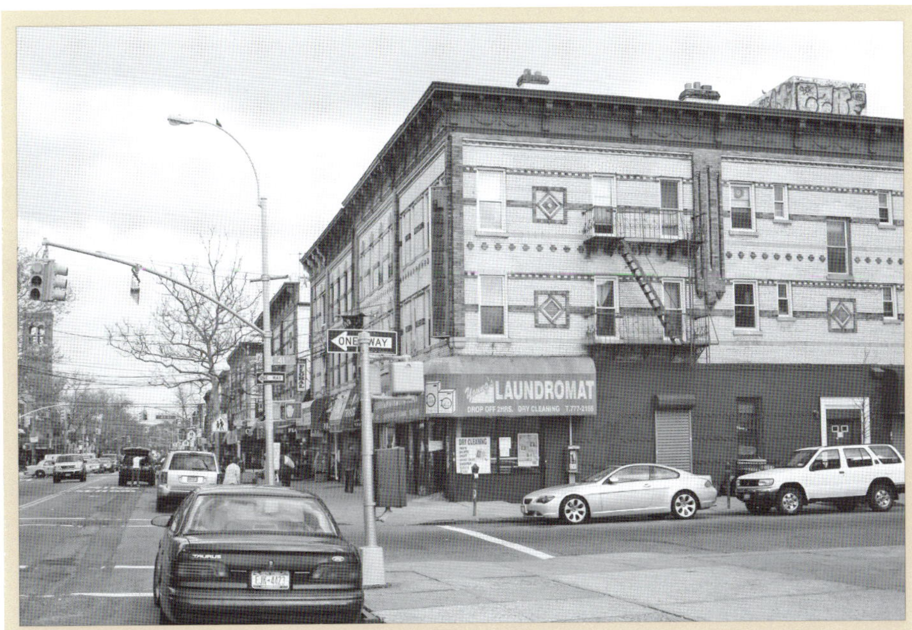

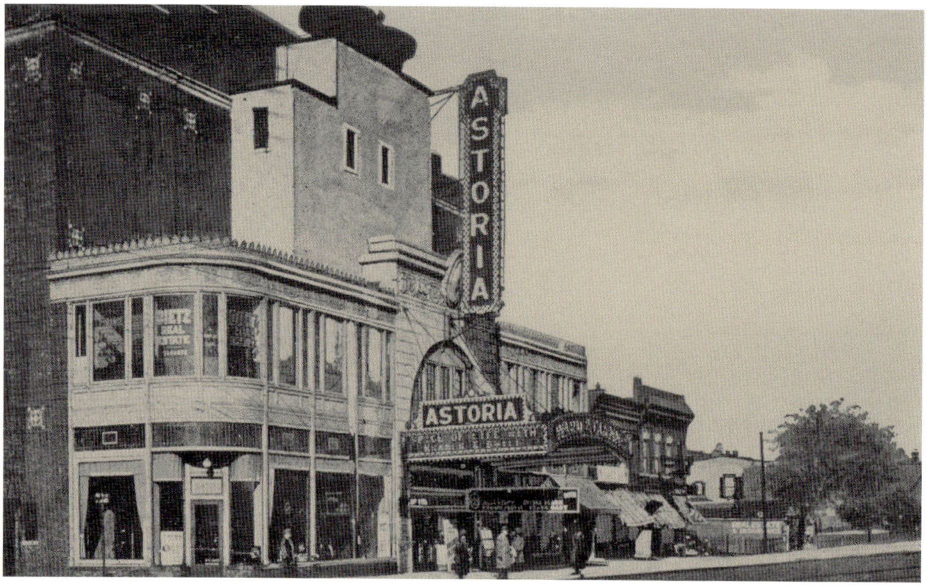

The community's first theater, Horak's Opera House, opened on Steinway Street in 1893. It was renamed the Arcade Theater and lasted until the 1920s. A block north was the Astoria Theater, and on the next block was the Triboro Theater. The Astoria, which seated 2,000, was designed by Thomas Lamb as a vaudeville house for the Ward and Glynne circuit (1920). Loew's acquired it in 1923. On December 26, 2001, the theater closed to become a gym and drugstore. (Then photograph courtesy Gary Vollo.)

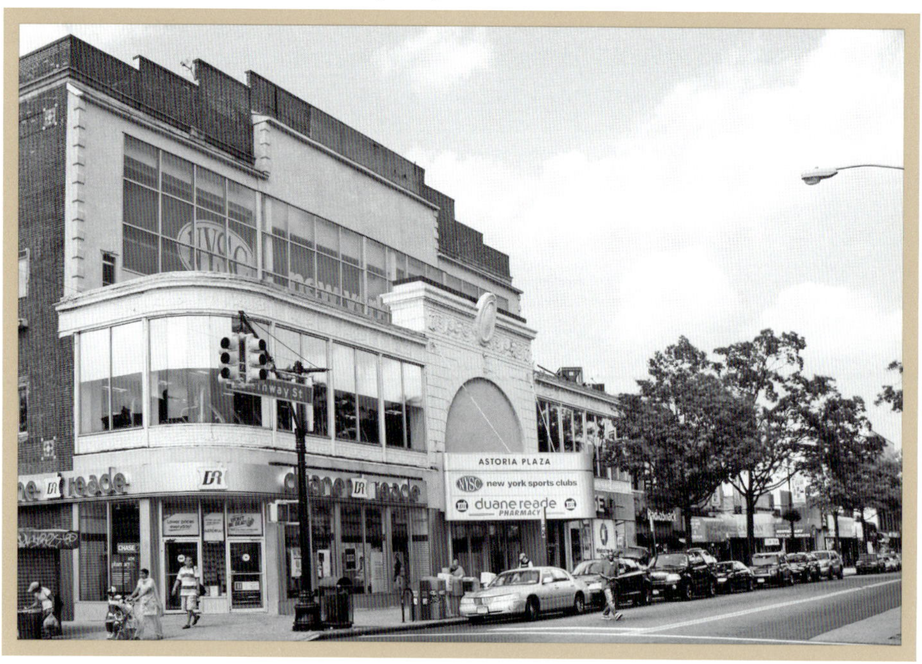

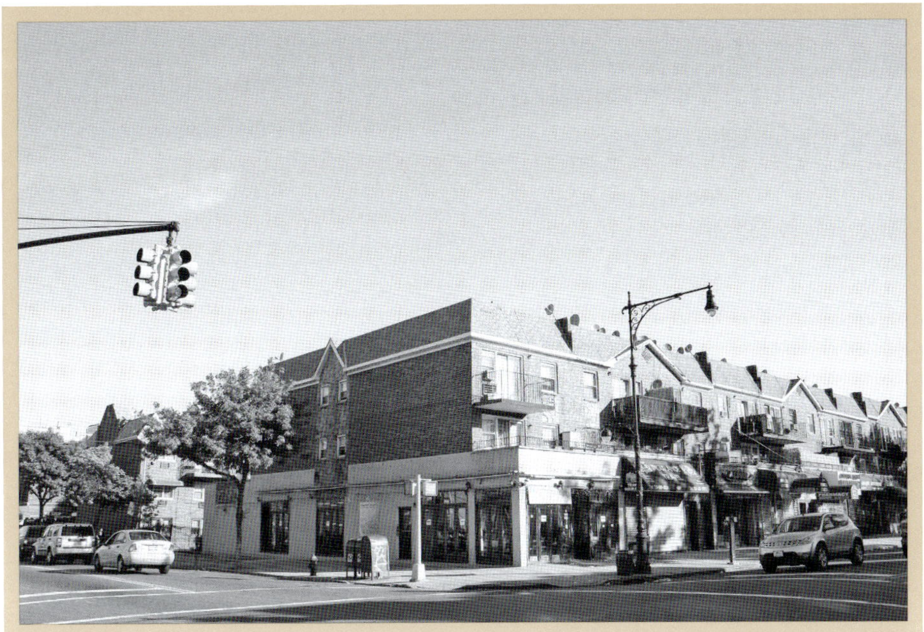

Opened in 1931, the Triboro was the last of the great movie palaces built by Thomas Lamb in New York City for the Loew's chain. It could seat nearly 3,300. The exterior was described as Mayan Revival and its palatial inside had an atmospheric-style ceiling. The theater drew audiences from around the borough. It was destroyed in 1974. Decades later, the community still laments this theater's passing.

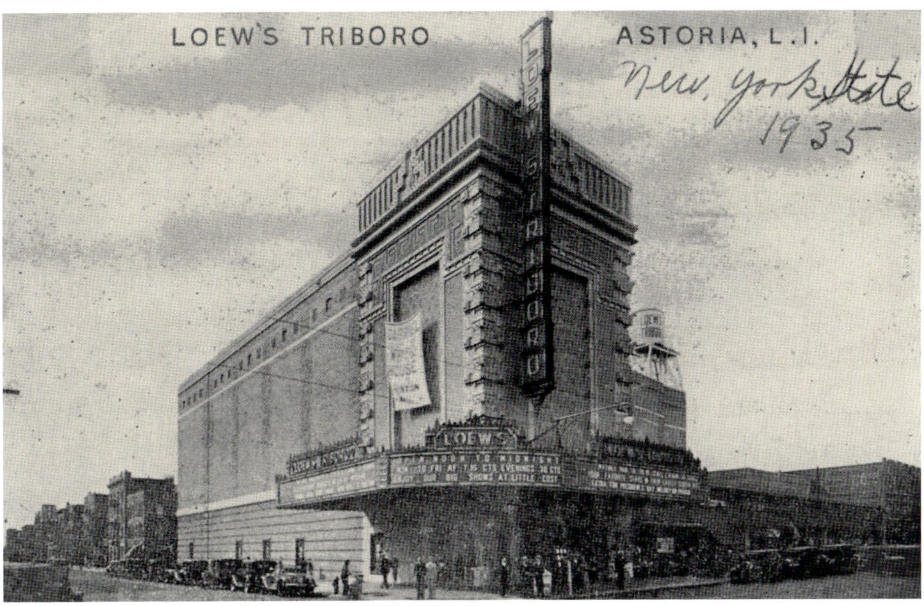

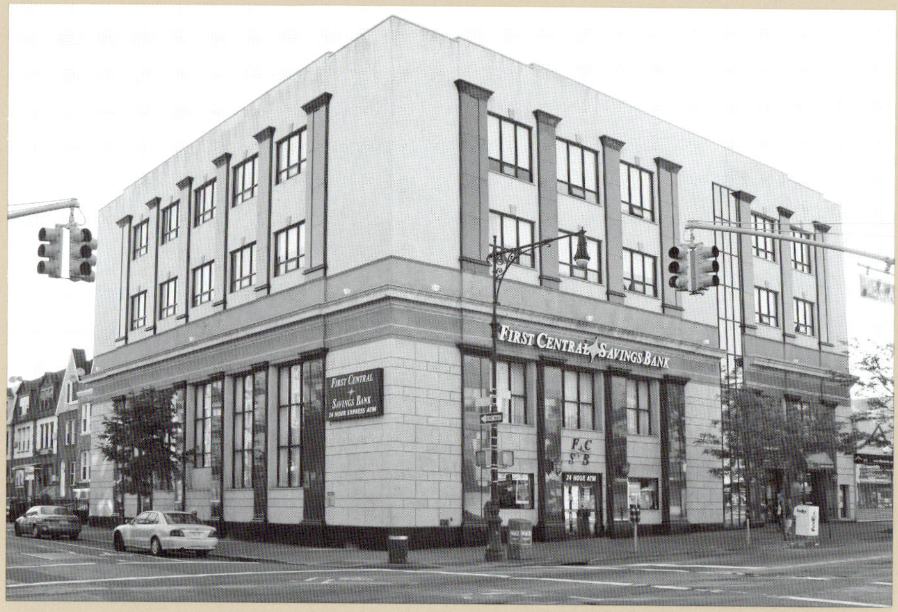

Organized in 1876, the Long Island City Savings Bank (later shortened to Long Island Savings Bank) built a number of offices as it followed the building boom in the 1920s. The bank later merged into a larger financial institution and sold off its branches. This formerly charming classical building on 30th Avenue had a delightful minipark next to it.

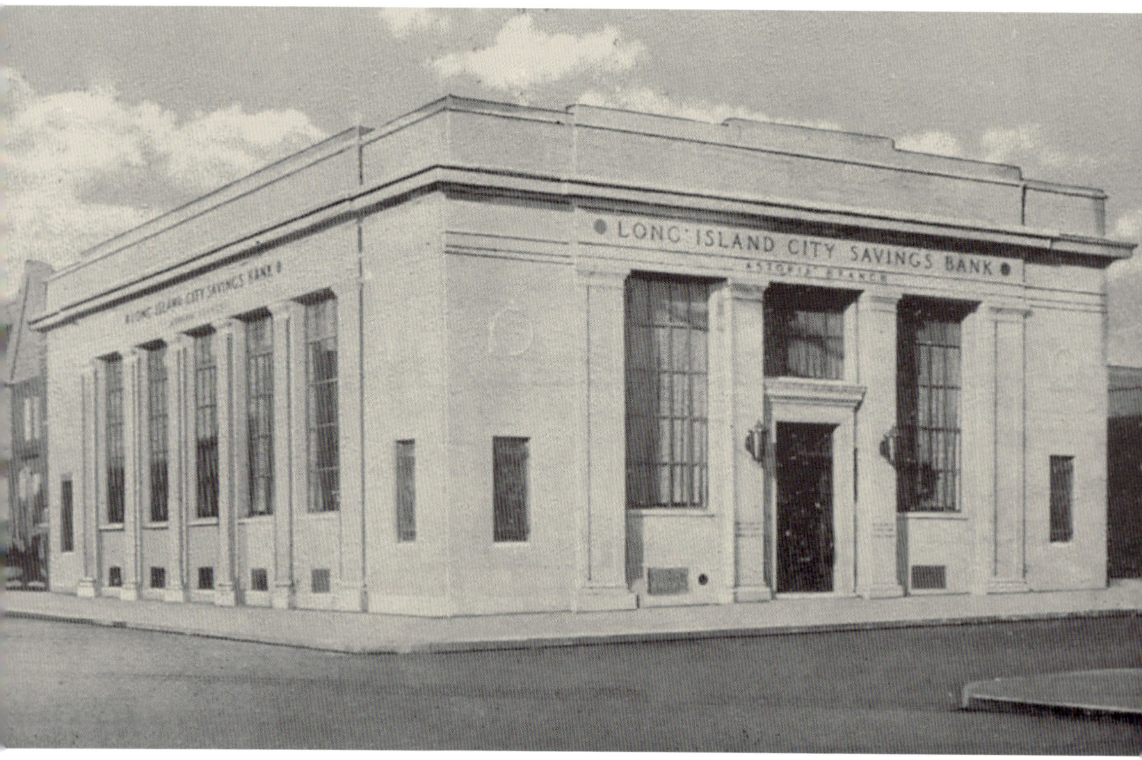

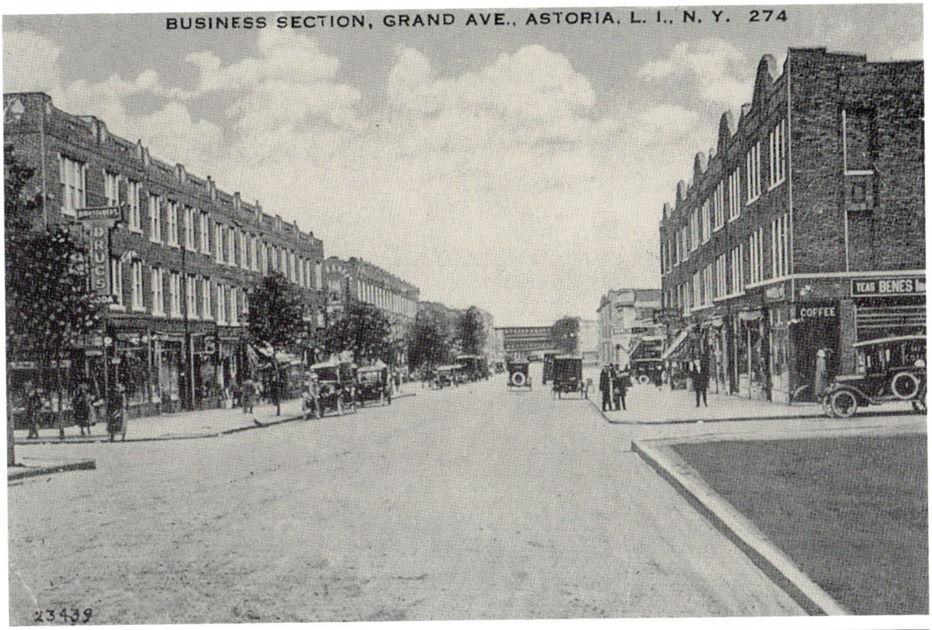

Growth on Grand (today 30th) Avenue was modest until the arrival of the elevated train in 1917. Like the neighboring Broadway station, yearly turnstile traffic jumped from 2 million to more than 5 million within 10 years. Lined today with cafés and specialty food stores, an address on this avenue continues to be in high demand.

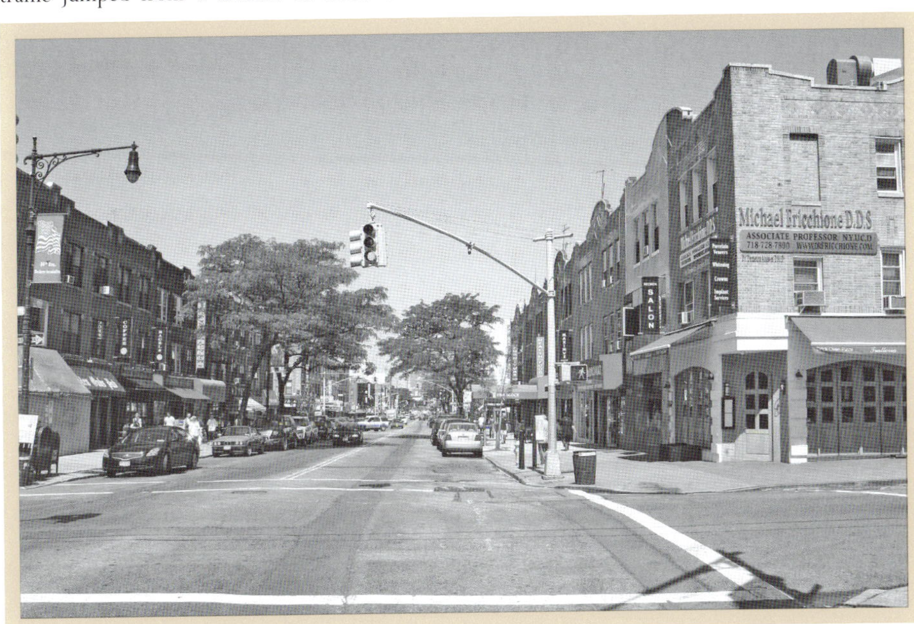

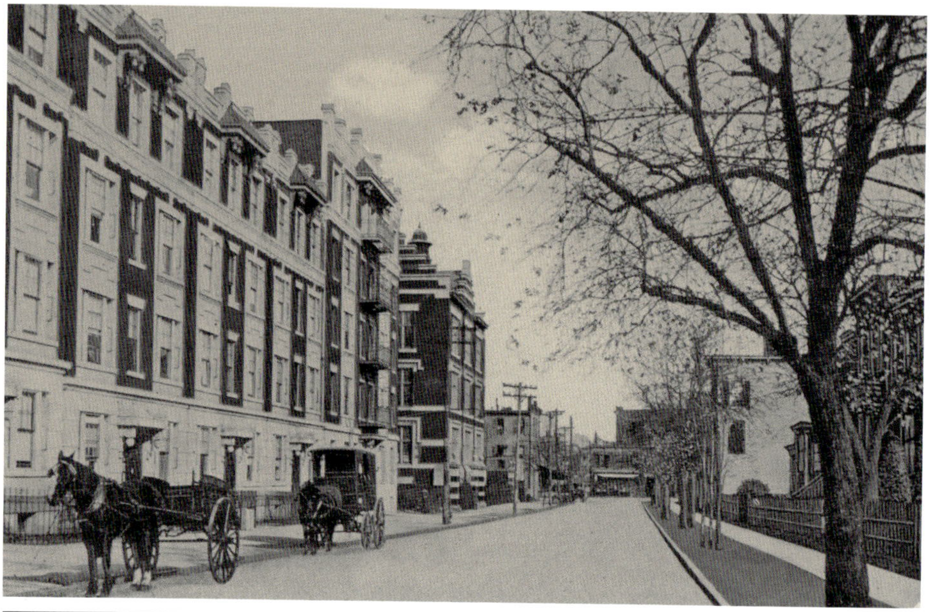

Buildings, particularly older ones constructed at a time when style and design were important, when permitted to keep that detail, contribute to the beauty of a block. This apartment building, with a pleasing design of brick and terra-cotta, earned immortality in a postcard. Except for the horse-drawn carriages, the block of 30th Street and 30th Avenue has remained virtually unchanged for nearly a century. (Then photograph courtesy Gary Vollo.)

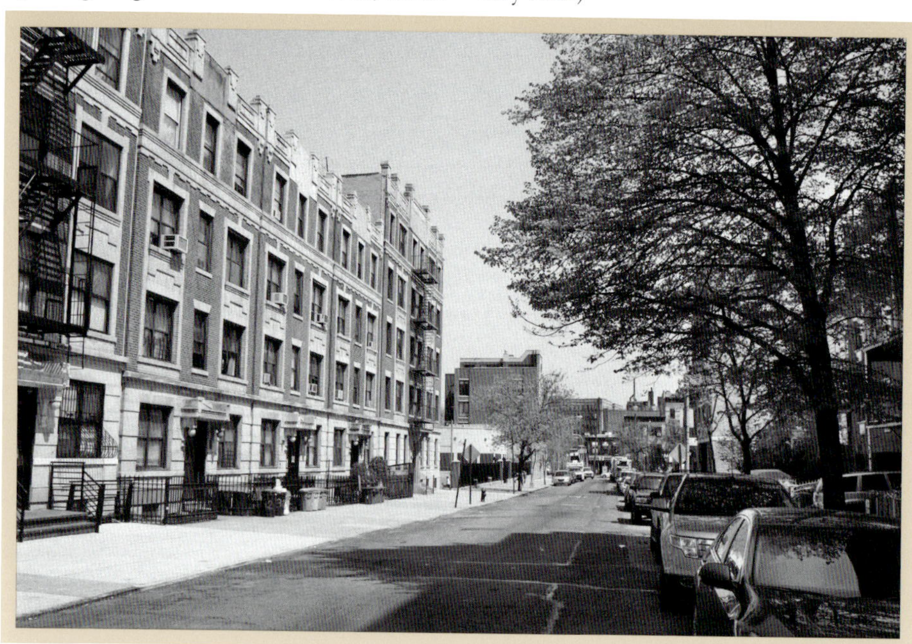

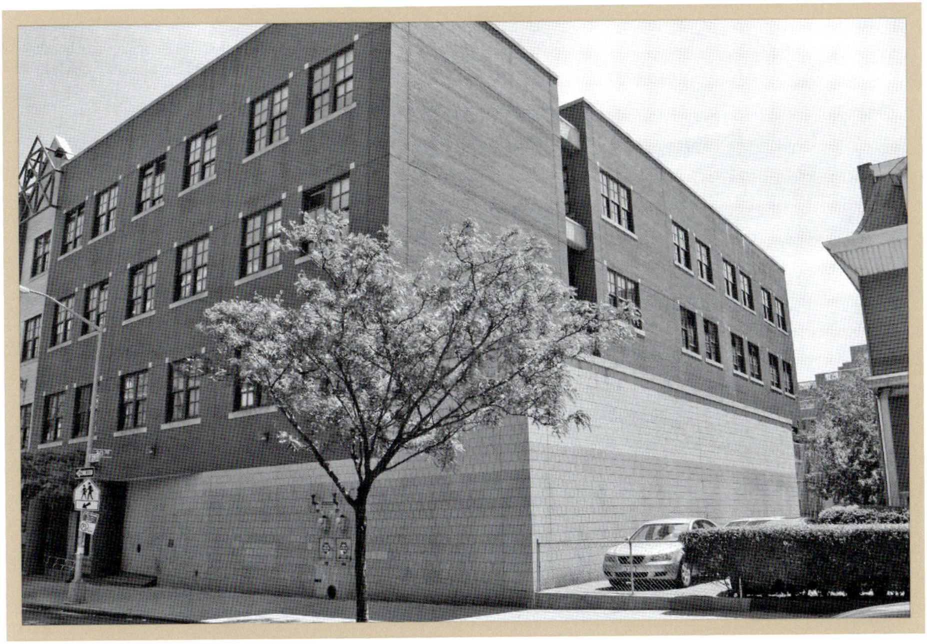

Fourth Ward Grammar School was on the east side of 29th Street and south of 30th Avenue. Built as a mansion by M. R. Sanford (1851) in the Greek revival style, it was later purchased by John E. Lockwood (1864). The building and the lot to the north were acquired in 1903 for a new school, P.S. 5. Note the house on the right in both pictures.

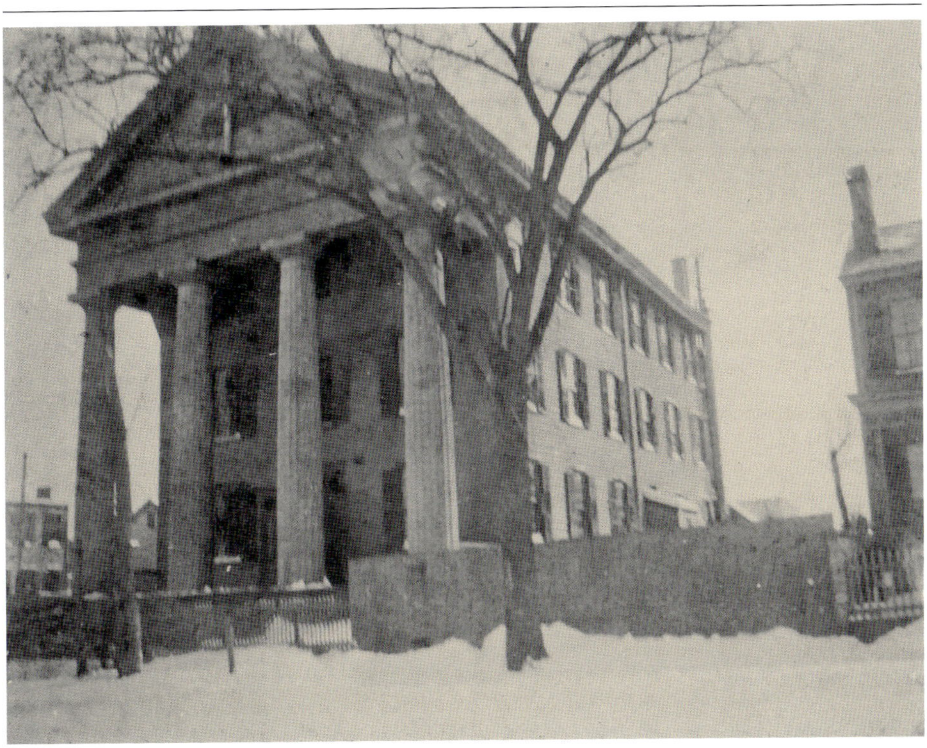

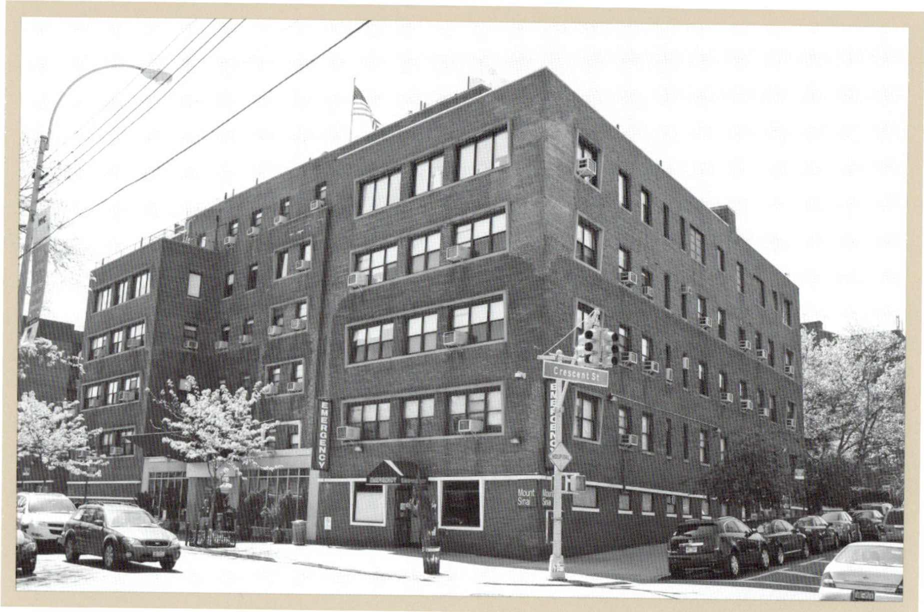

The original Astoria Hospital (1891) started as a charity of Mrs. F. E. Hagemeyer, a wealthy parishioner of St. George's church in Astoria. After opening an even larger facility in 1896, it was forced to close when the city refused to give it financial support. Astoria General Hospital opened as Daly's Astoria Sanitorium in 1910. It is the modest stucco building to the right, and it still stands.

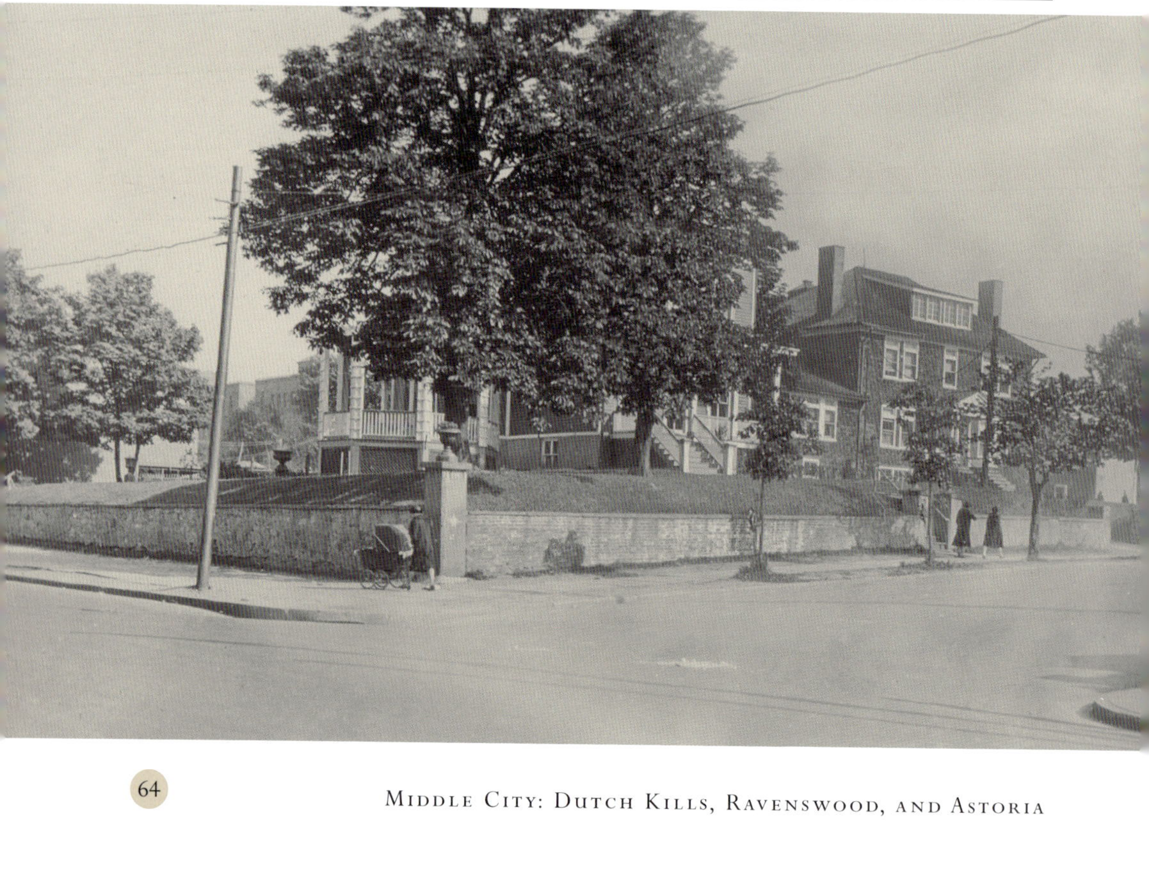

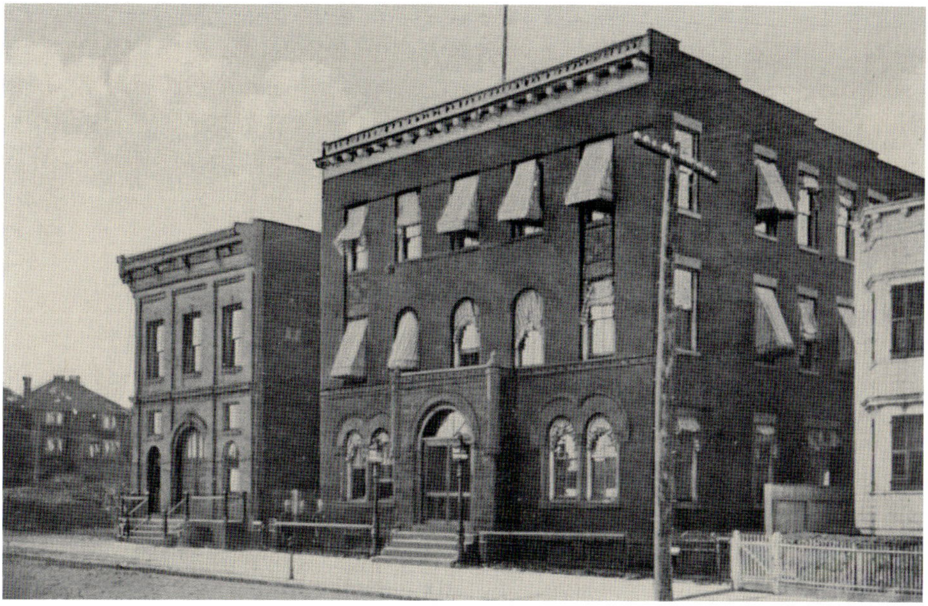

The Astoria Precinct (today the 114th Precinct) was one of two precincts in Long Island City. When it opened in the 1890s, it had two acting sergeants, two roundsmen, and 33 patrolmen. The smaller building on the left was the Astoria Veteran Firemen Association, a group that traced its roots to the Village of Astoria Fire Department. Before the firemen's association disappeared, some time before 1950, it sold the building to a chapter of the Veterans of Foreign Wars. Both buildings are on 30th Avenue. The police have moved to newer quarters, and the firehouse is now medical offices. (Then photograph courtesy Gary Vollo.)

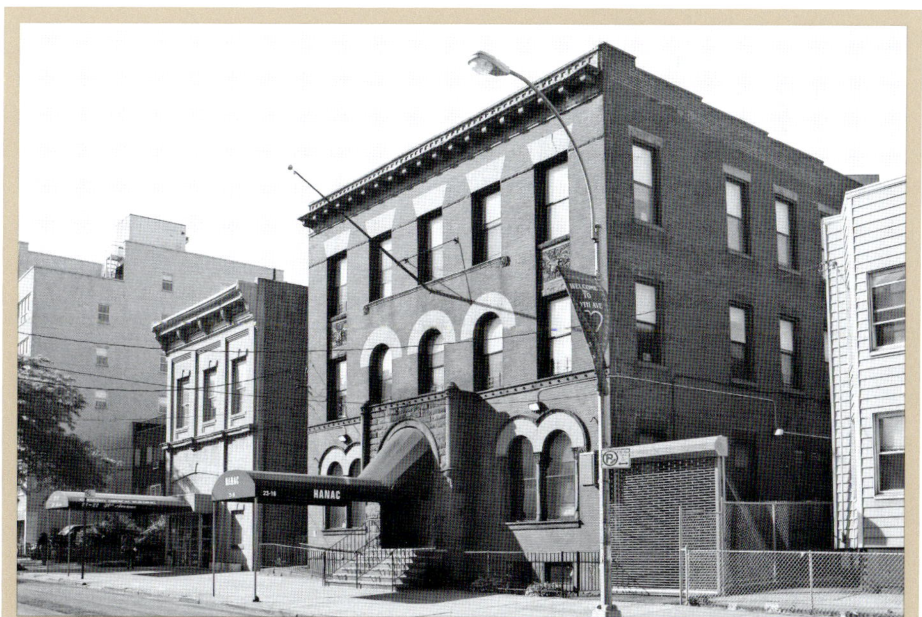

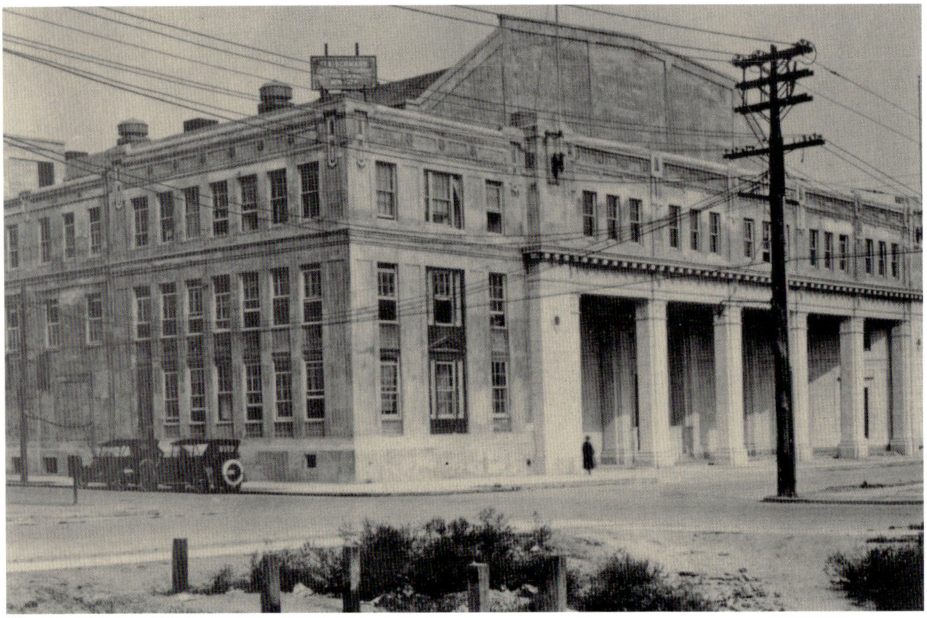

These buildings went by many names: Famous Players–Lasky Studios, Paramount Studios, Army Pictorial Center, and finally, Kaufman-Astoria Studios. The facility is one of the largest film and television production studios in the country. *Sesame Street* and the *Cosby Show*, among many others, were produced on the same stages that were once home in the 1920s and 1930s to Marx Brothers comedies, Rudolph Valentino romances, and Busby Berkeley musicals. (Then photograph courtesy Kaufman-Astoria Studios.)

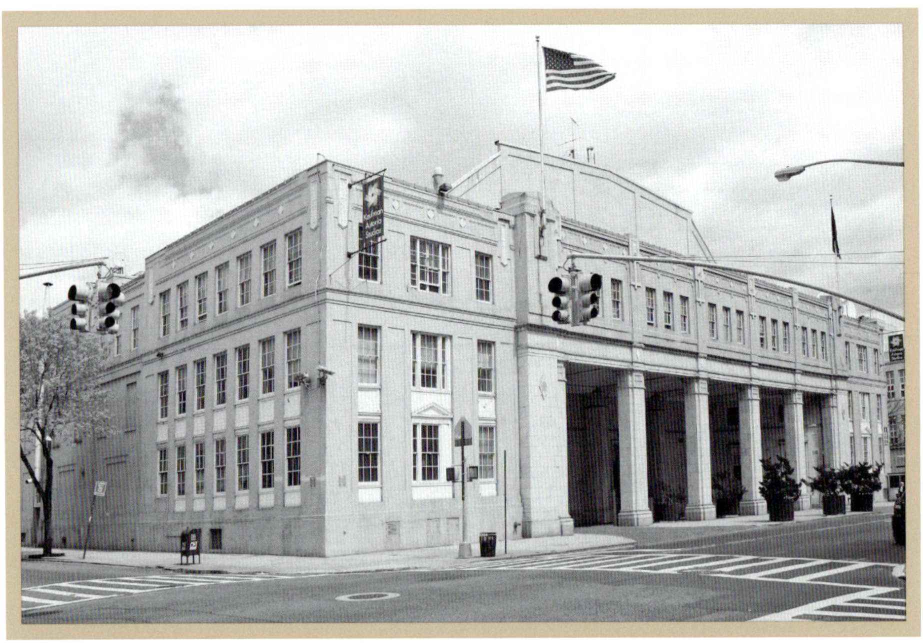

CHAPTER 3

UPPER CITY

OLD ASTORIA, DITMARS, AND STEINWAY

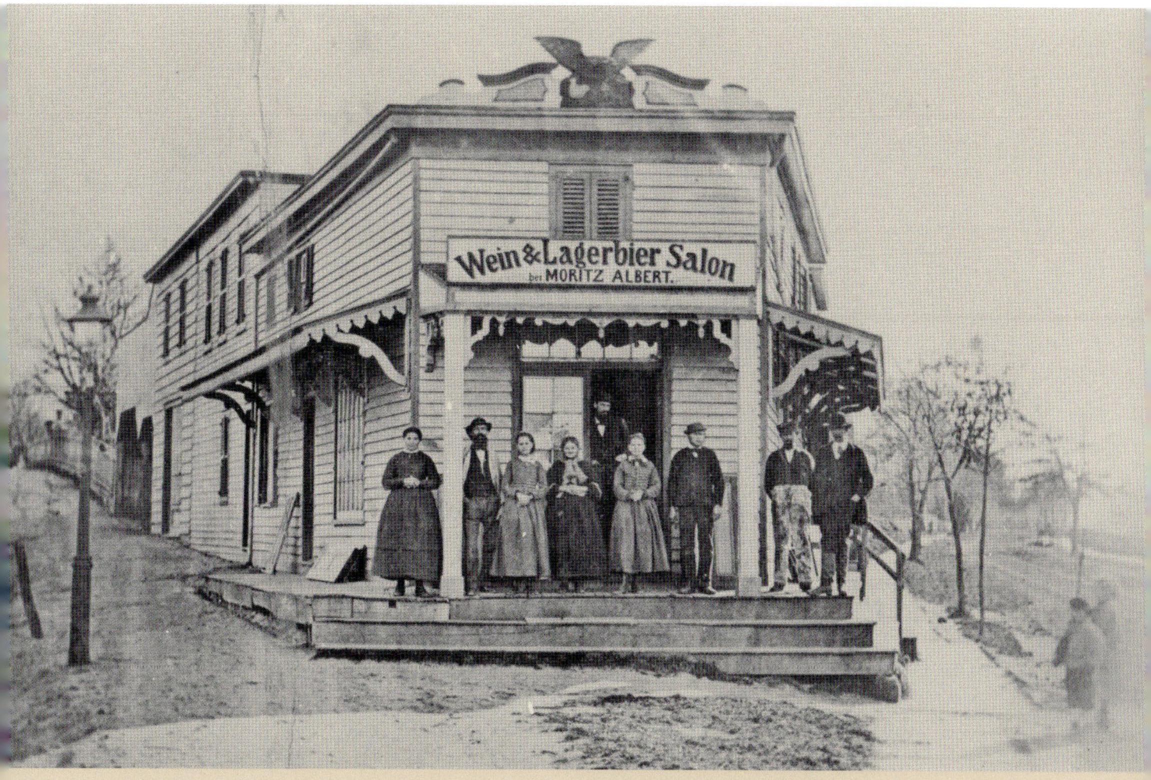

At Astoria Square, Albert Moritz—and perhaps his family—proudly stands in front of his saloon at the corner of Astoria Boulevard and 27th Avenue. Dated around 1875, it is one of the earliest images of Old Astoria Village. The Astoria "Flatiron Building" was later at this location. Old Astoria Village is a noteworthy historic district in New York City. (Courtesy Queens Borough Public Library–Long Island Division, Eugene L. Armbruster Photographs.)

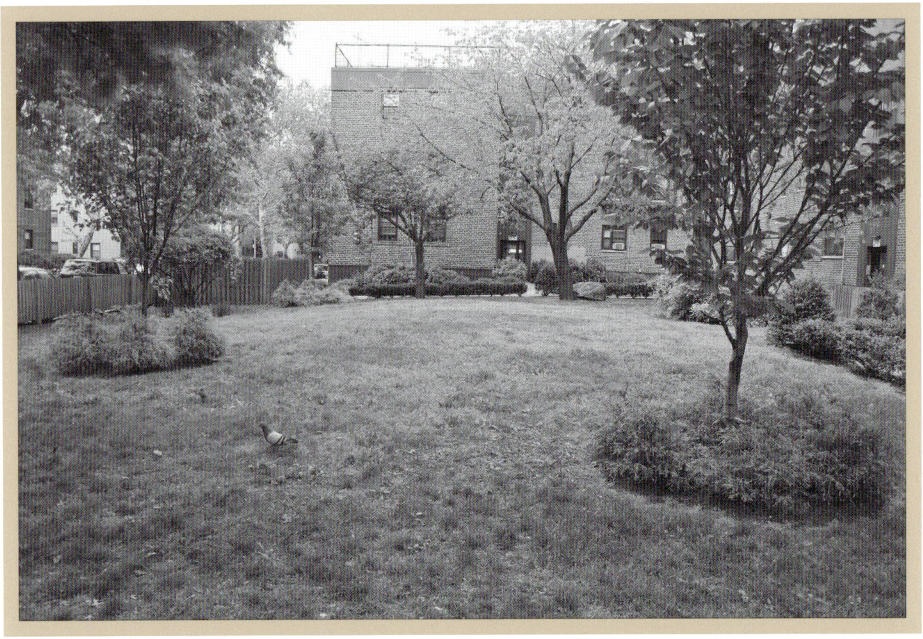

The Rapalye Burying Ground was just north and west of the corner of 21st Avenue and 21st Street. This cemetery was behind the Polhemus House on Shore Boulevard, earlier the Rapalye family home (see page 88). As late as 1904, there were eight stones of the Brinckerhoff, Rapalye, and Sheffield families with dates from 1776 to 1830. Two burials, Jacob Rapalye and his wife, Sarah, died within six weeks of each other during the turbulent year of 1776. Both tombstones were inscribed in Dutch.

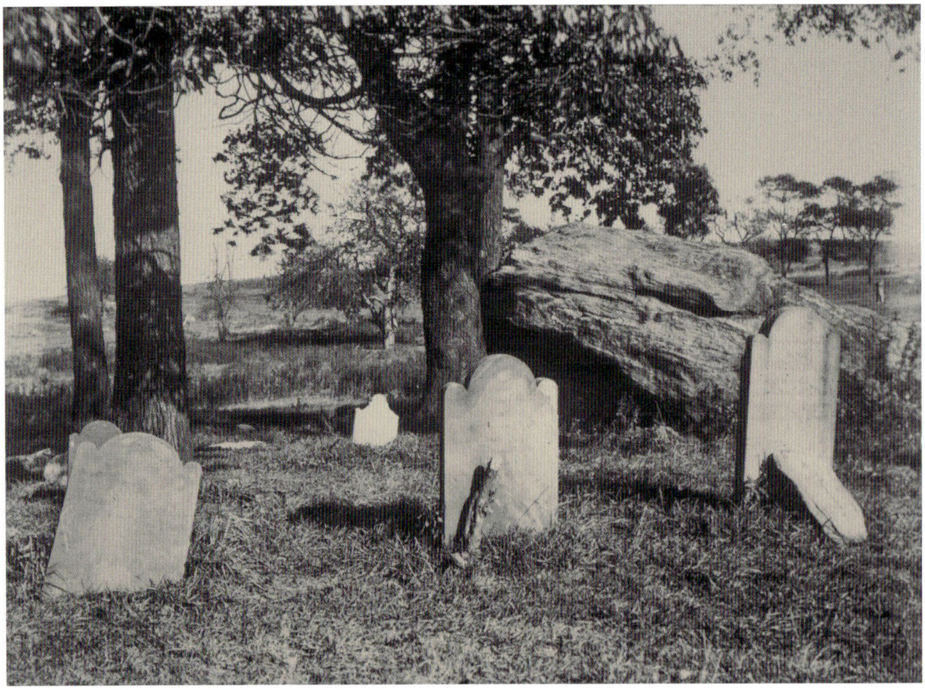

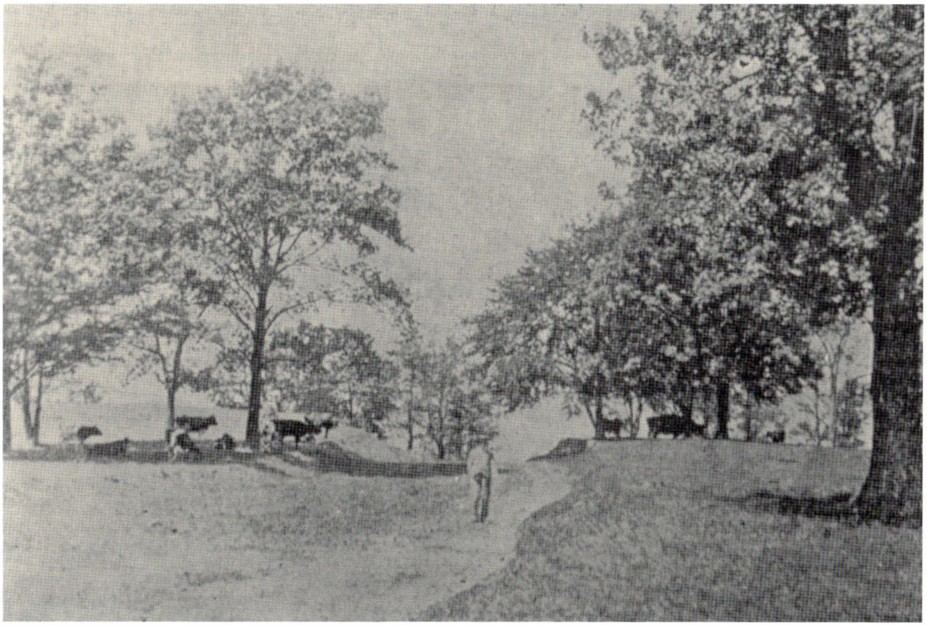

Cornelius Berrien bought Berrien's Island and the land adjacent to it in 1727. In 1853, the 400-acre Berrien estate, called Casina (Latin for "small cabin"), was sold to Edward Woolsey. Woolsey enjoyed playing the role of gentleman farmer raising thoroughbred horses and cattle. After his death, it was sold in 1898 to the Consolidated Gas and Astoria Light, Heat, and Power Company. This is now a power plant on 20th Avenue at the East River.

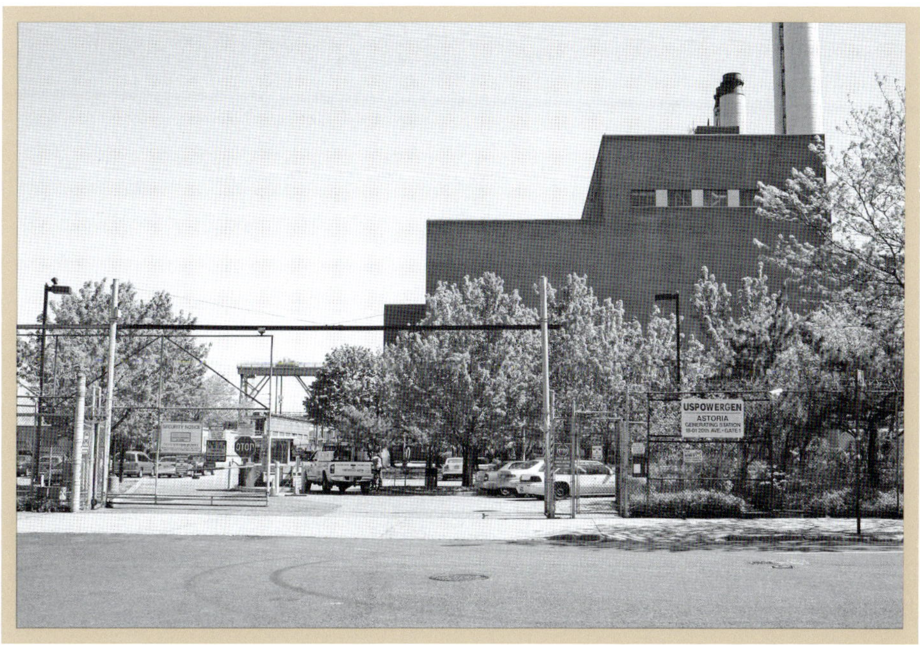

Between 1850 and 1880, William C. Wilson ran a large commercial florist operation at Astoria Boulevard. His 8-acre field of tuberoses would frequently ship as many as 100,000 flowers at a time to the New York market. William Steinway bought out the Wilson estate (1890) and tore down the only windmill in western Queens. (Then photograph courtesy Queens Borough Public Library–Long Island Division, Illustrations Collection—Astoria.)

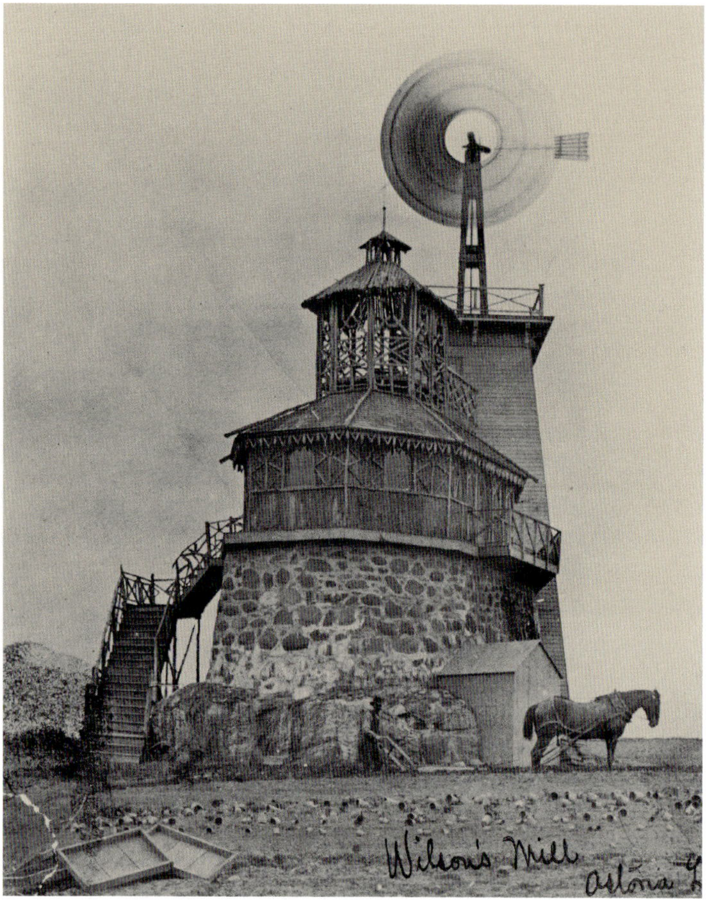

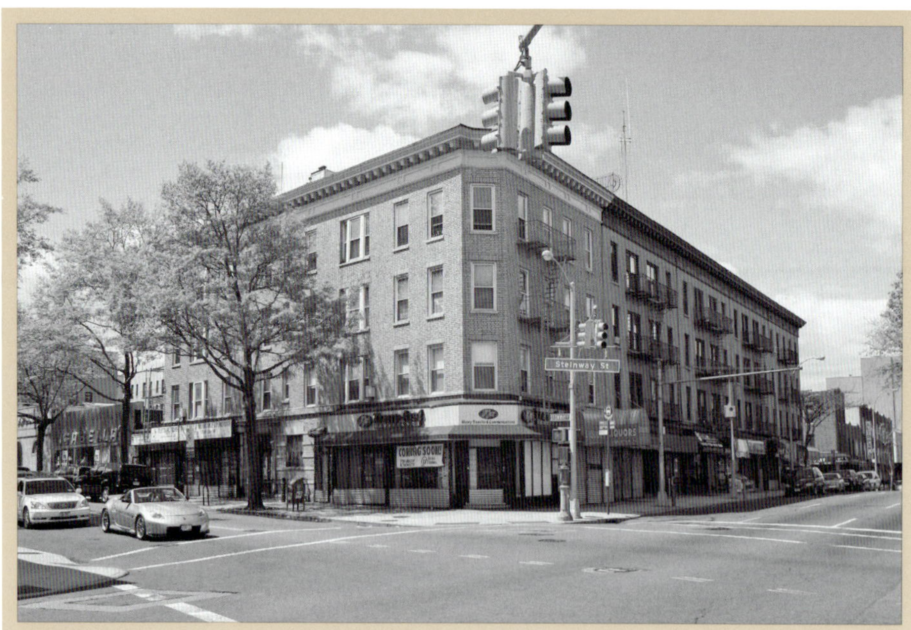

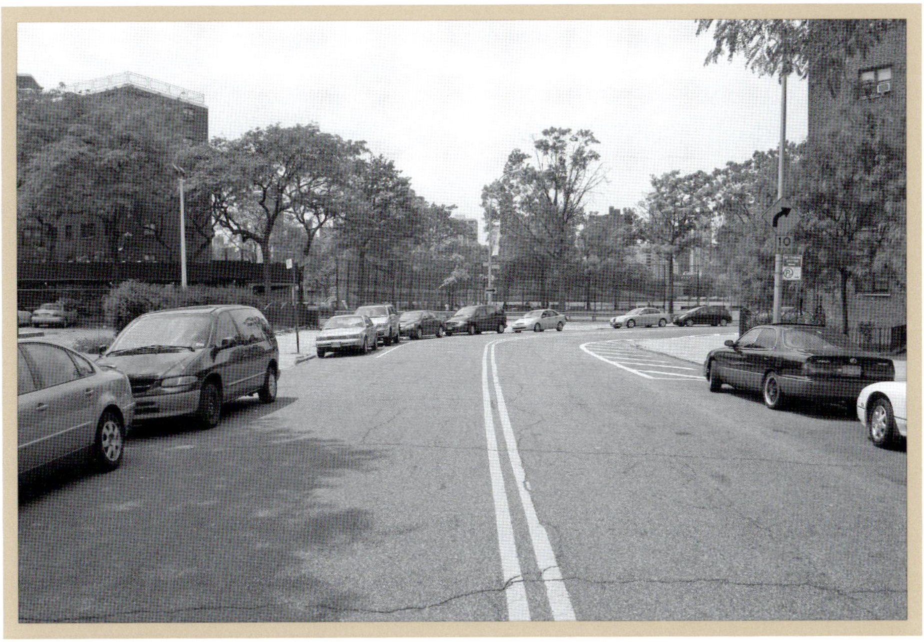

The Hell Gate Ferry, or later the Astoria Ferry, was one of the two oldest ferries between Manhattan and Long Island (the other was the Brooklyn ferry). The boat was summoned by ringing a large bell. Steamboat service (1840s) made nine daily trips from Peck Slip to Astoria, charging a 10¢ fare. Service was changed from 86th to 92nd Street (1890s). The ferry was discontinued when the Triborough (Robert F. Kennedy) Bridge opened (1936), and the location was obliterated in building the Astoria Houses (1940s).

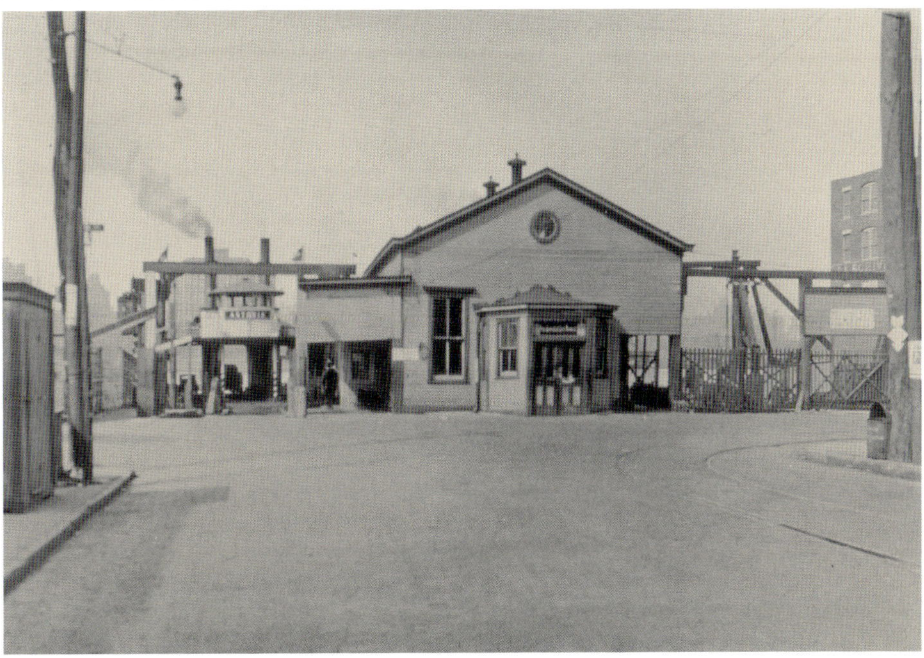

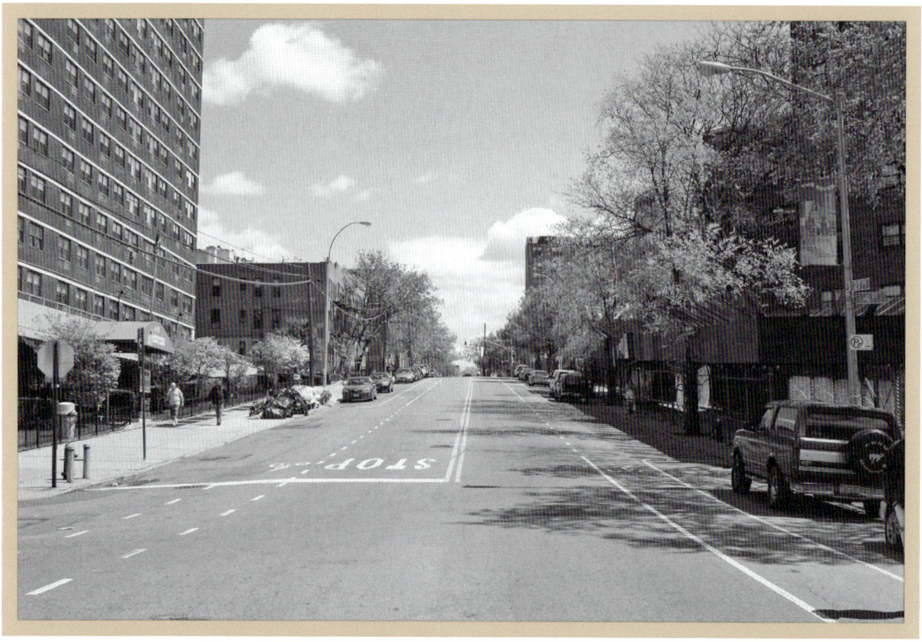

For two generations, from 1840 to about 1900, Old Astoria Village was a suburban retreat for wealthy commuters as well as home to people who worked at the ferry, the waterfront, and in local carpet and silk weaving factories. "The Hill," the village's social and cultural center, was the stretch of 27th Avenue that ran from 2nd Street to 14th Street. Everything on the right of the photograph was cleared for the Astoria Houses by 1950. (Then photograph courtesy Bob Stonehill.)

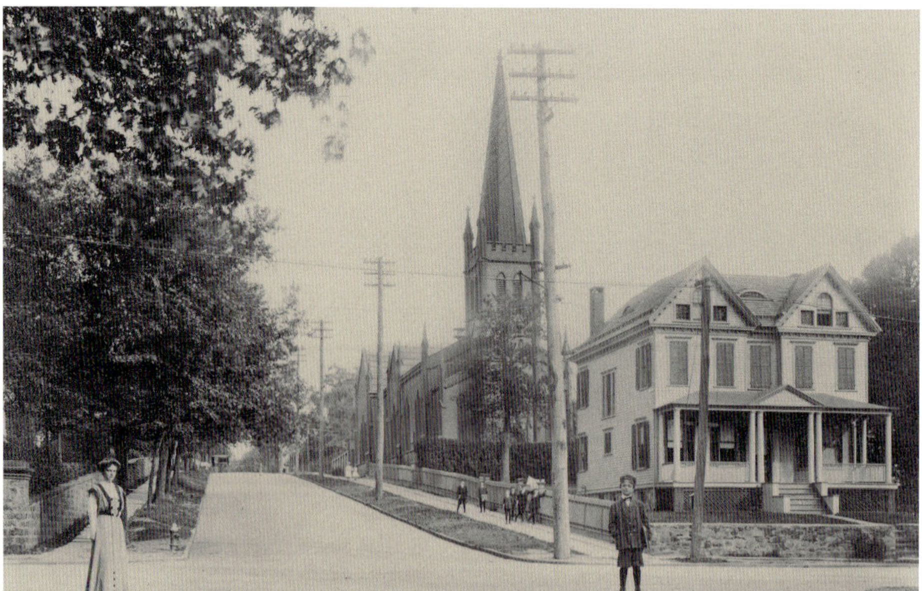

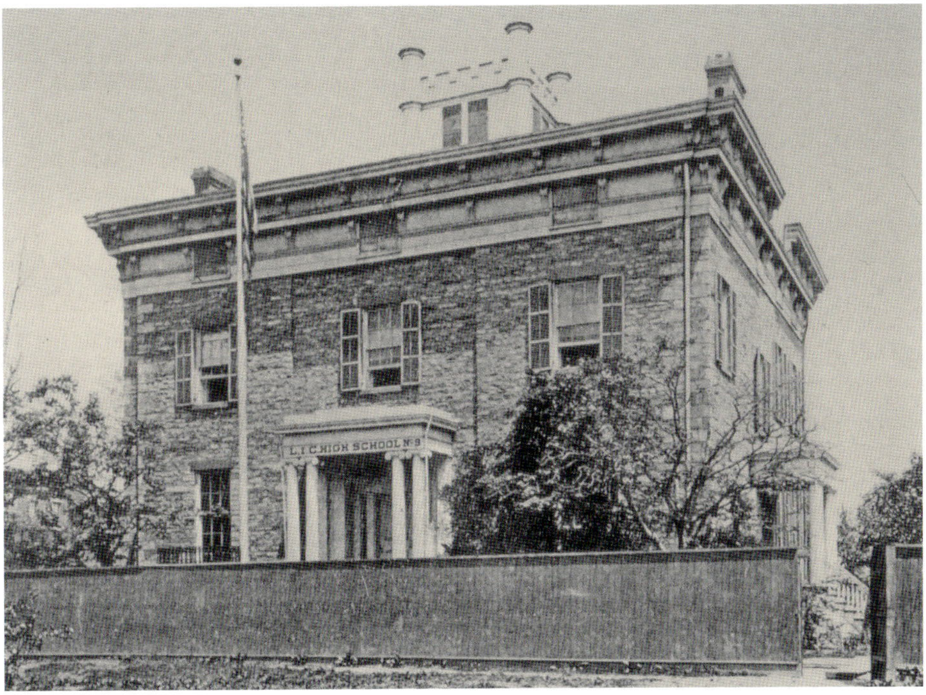

The stone house of Stephen Halsey (1840) stood at 2nd Street and Astoria Boulevard. He sold it to Marcena Monson (1850). The stone was quarried locally, and its foundation was 4 feet thick, the walls were 2 feet thick, and the seven rooms on the first floor had 18-foot ceilings lit by 14-foot windows. Long Island City purchased the mansion in 1893 and converted it into P.S. 9, the Long Island City High School. The building was torn down in the 1940s to build the Astoria Houses.

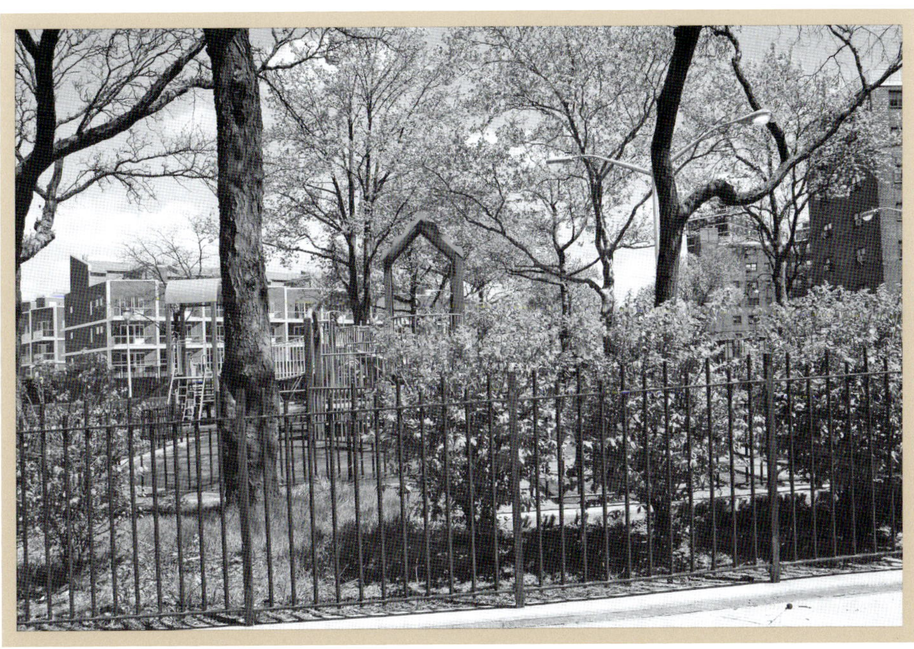

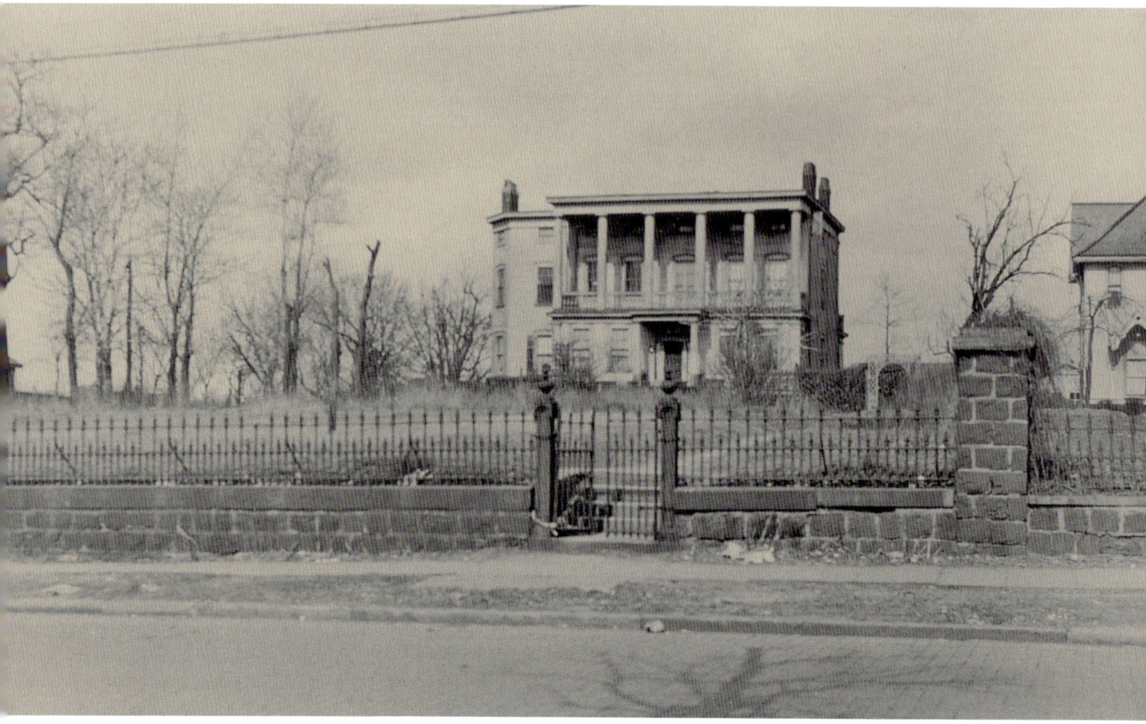

North of 27th Avenue and well back from the street was the home of Josiah Blackwell, a dry goods merchant from New York who built it around 1850. The historic photographs of Old Astoria Village reveal that the community once had one of New York City's largest collections of freestanding mansions. They were built just before the Civil War, at a time when eclectic architectural styles were popular.

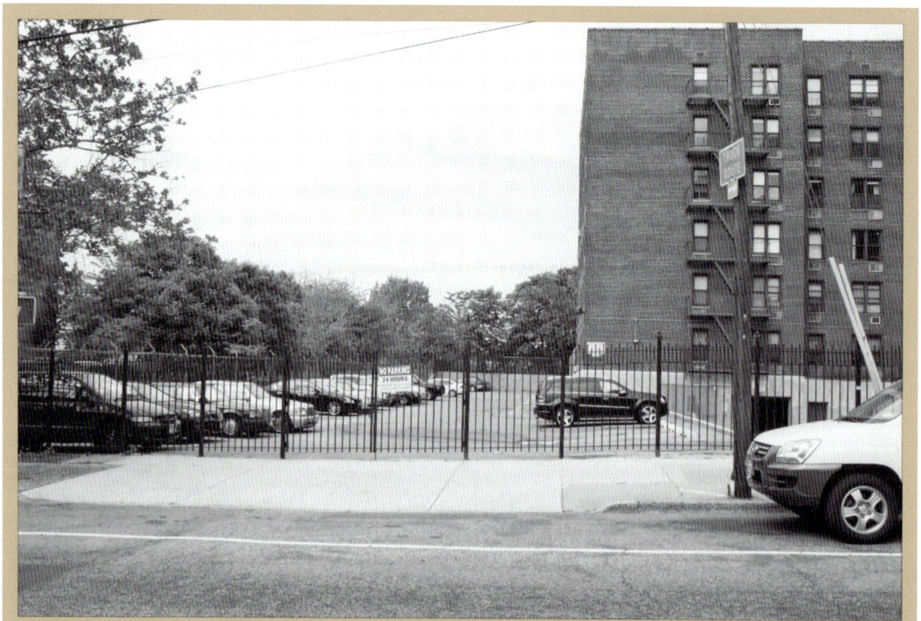

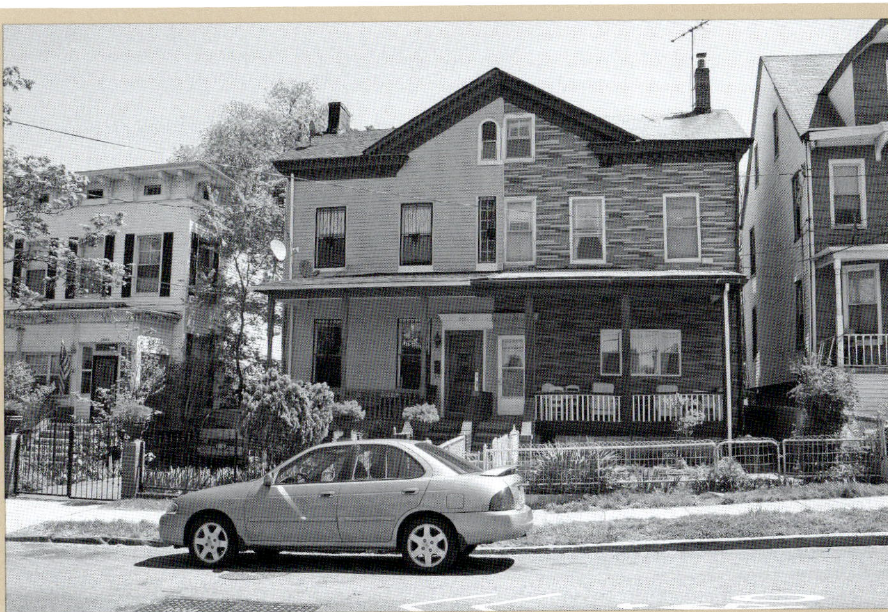

On 9th Street, a *c.* 1870 mansion was sold decades ago to two individual owners who each had differing tastes (and budgets) for home décor. Although a few historic buildings are destroyed each year, the area still has enough fascinating structures to make it one of the most interesting neighborhoods in the city for the urban explorer. Hidden gems like this can be found from the East River to 21st Street and from Astoria Park South to 30th Road.

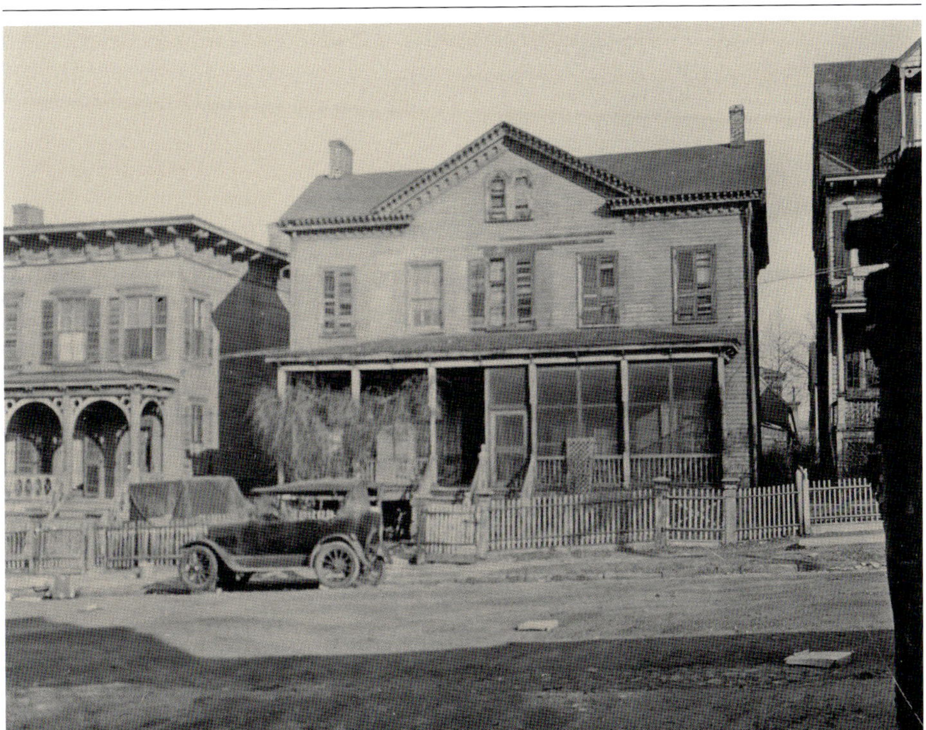

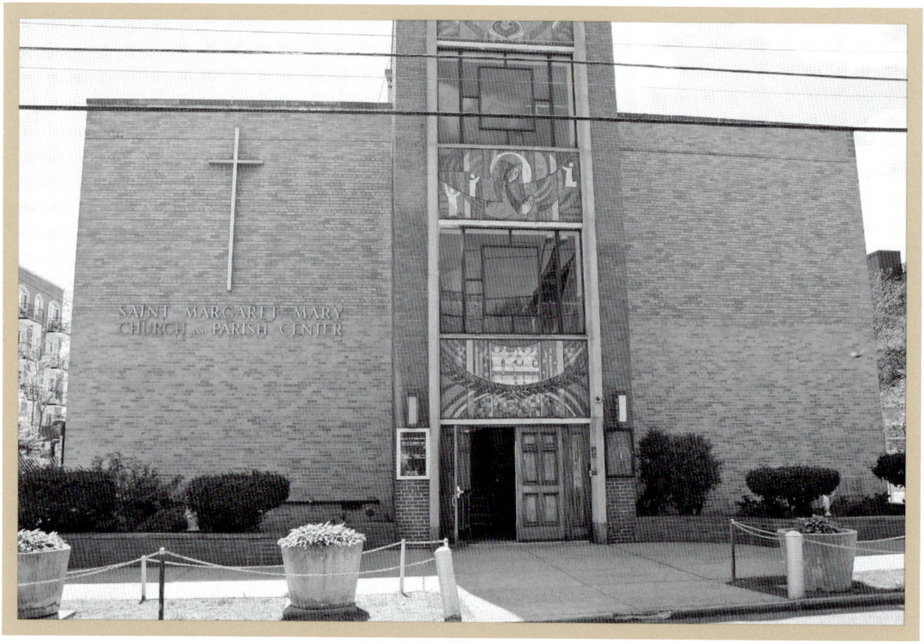

Patriarch Samuel Blackwell, owner of much of Astoria in the early 19th century, had 16 children. They married into local families, making a good number of Astoria's elite part of their extended dynasty. The Blackwells also once owned Ravenswood and Blackwells (today Roosevelt) Island. The Blackwell homestead (pictured) was modeled after an old Southern planter's mansion. It had a fabulous view in the center of a large parcel of land and occupied the highest ground on "The Hill," today 27th Avenue. (Then photograph courtesy Bob Stonehill.)

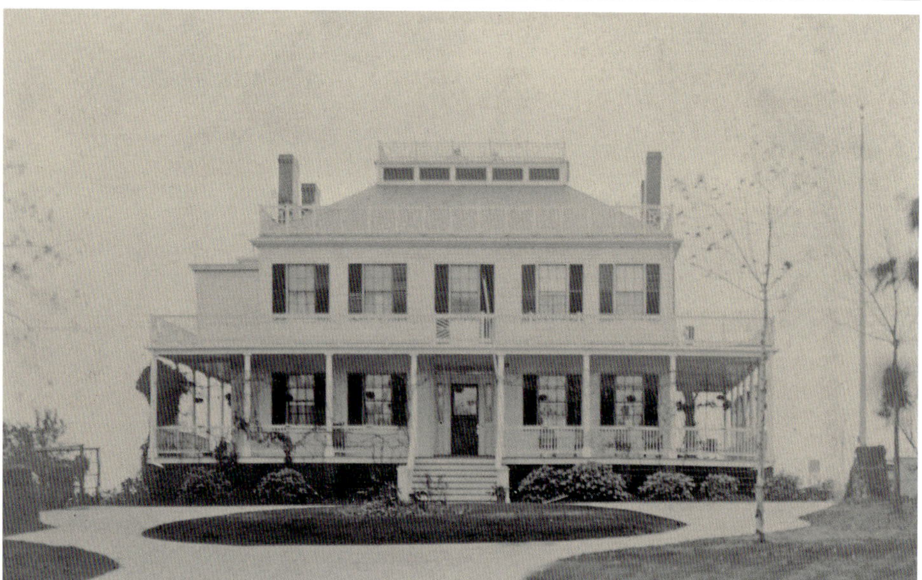

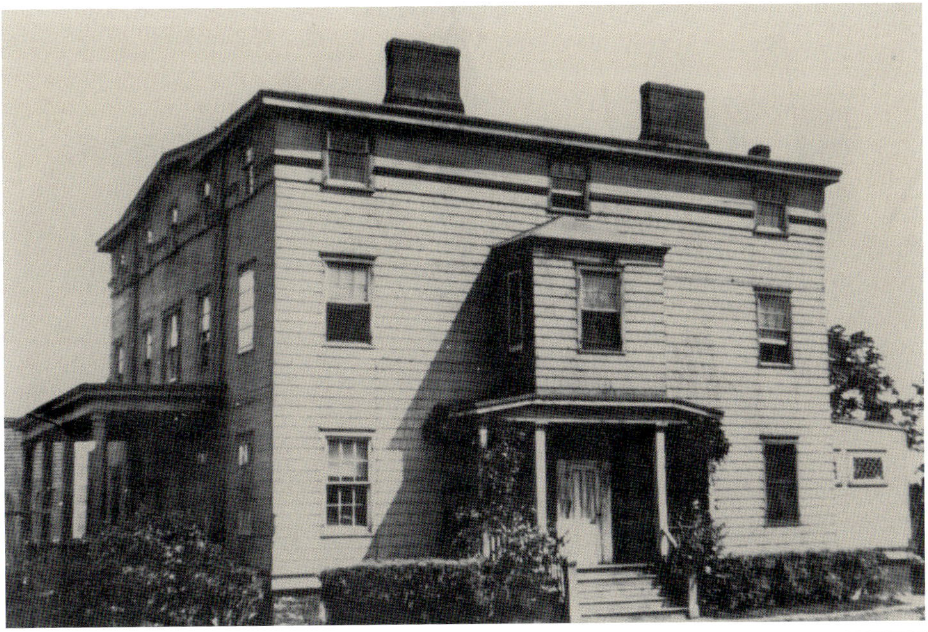

The Astoria Institute (1828) originally was to be a "female seminary" or boarding school for young ladies. Local supporters sought financial backing from John Jacob Astor, even offering to rename Hallets Cove Astoria. They went ahead with this name change even after Astor gave them a disappointing few hundred dollars. The building became the parsonage for St. George's church in the 1890s. The Landmarks Preservation Commission rejected an application in 2004, claiming that it did not meet the criteria for designation. It was demolished in 2006.

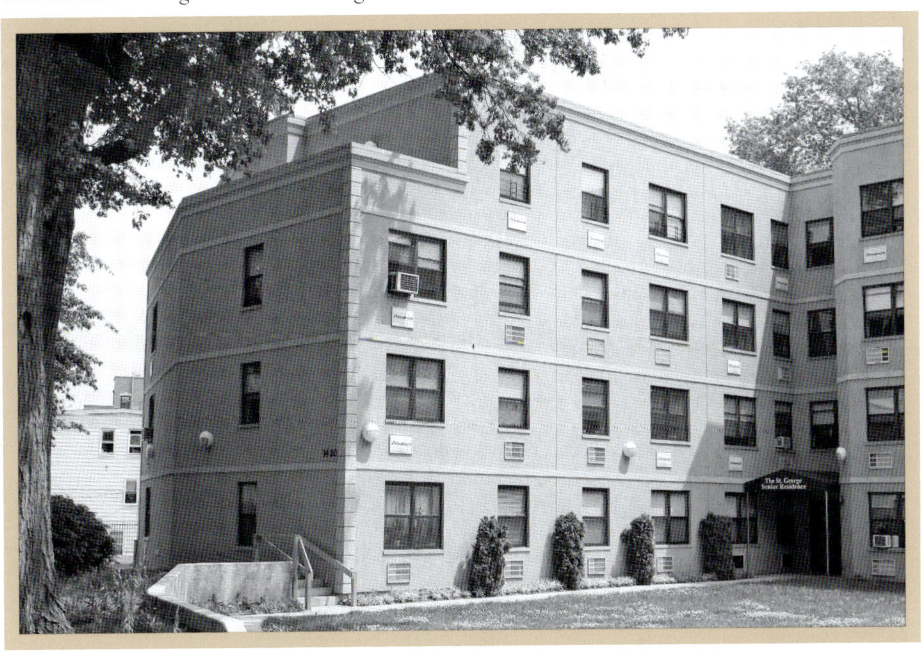

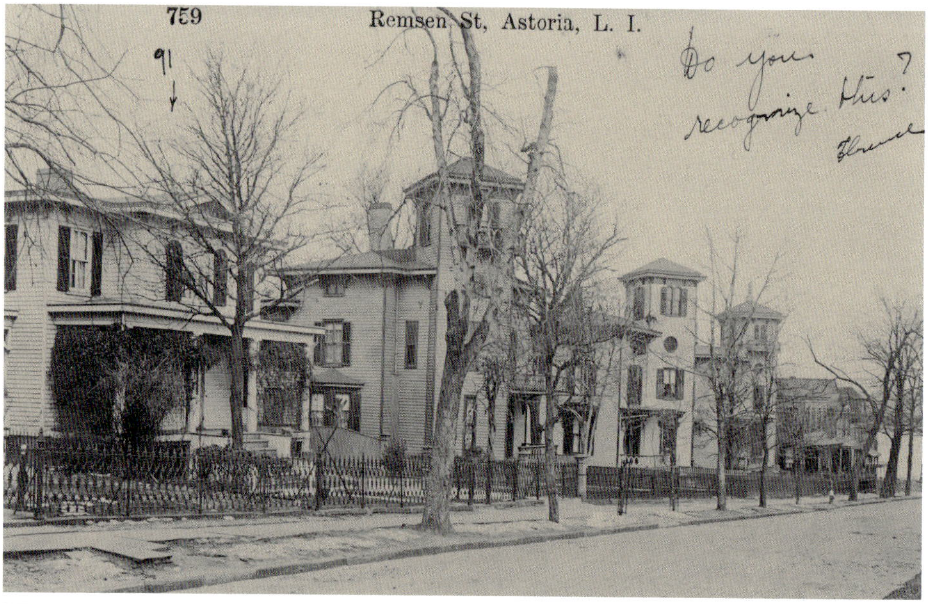

As late as the 1970s, Remsen (today 12th) Street was lined with mansions that were between 100 and 150 years old. As of this writing (2010), only one house remains in this view. Dozens of landmark-worthy buildings still stand within the community, but every application for designation by the Landmarks Preservation Commission has been rejected to date.

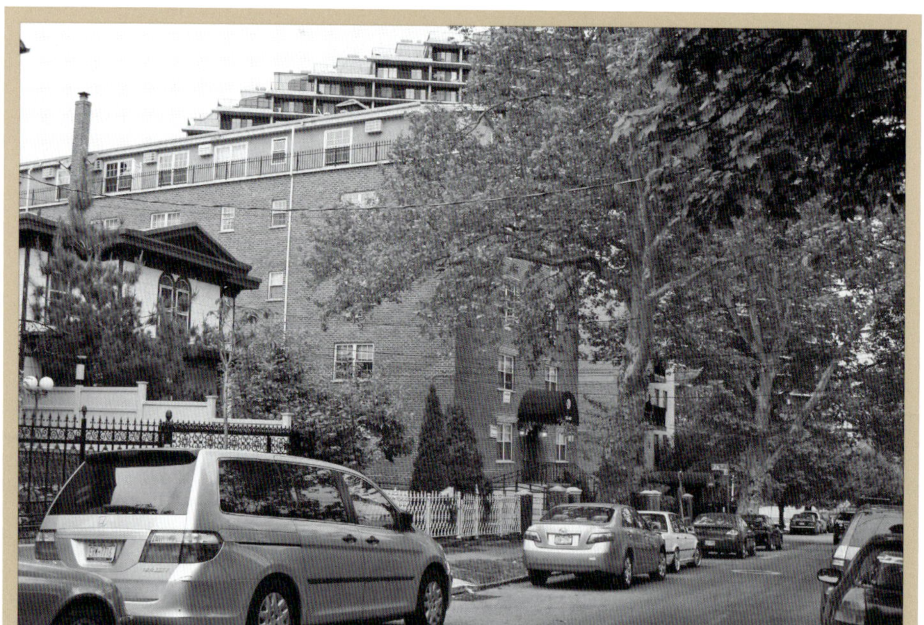

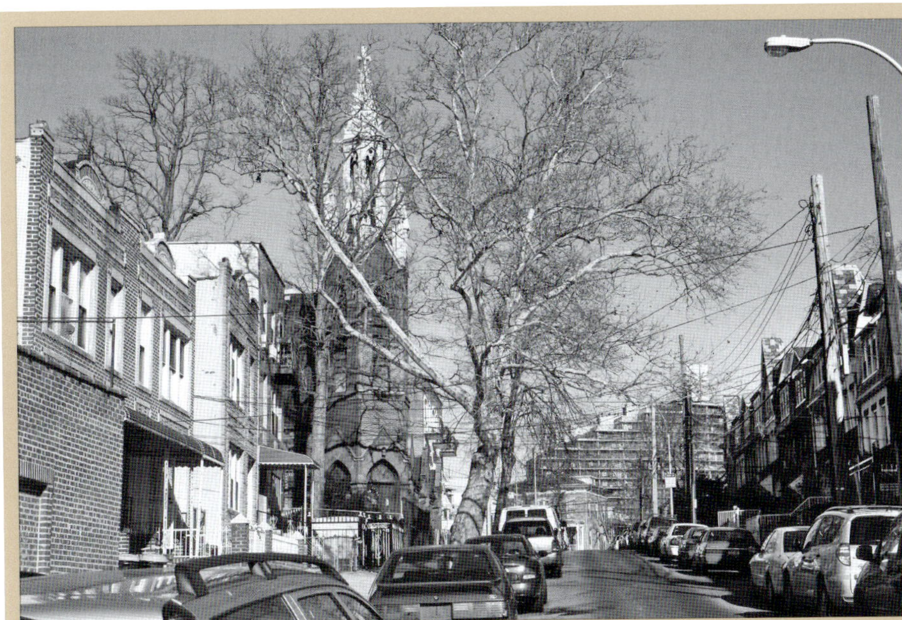

The Reformed Church of Astoria, organized in 1835, laid the cornerstone for its first building on 14th Street the following year. The church suffered a fire in 1888 but was quickly rebuilt and dedicated a year later. Its steeple, once taller, was damaged after being struck by lightning. On its grounds are monuments from a former cemetery. One is the family vault of Stephen Halsey, who is still remembered as the "Father of Astoria." (Then photograph courtesy Gary Vollo.)

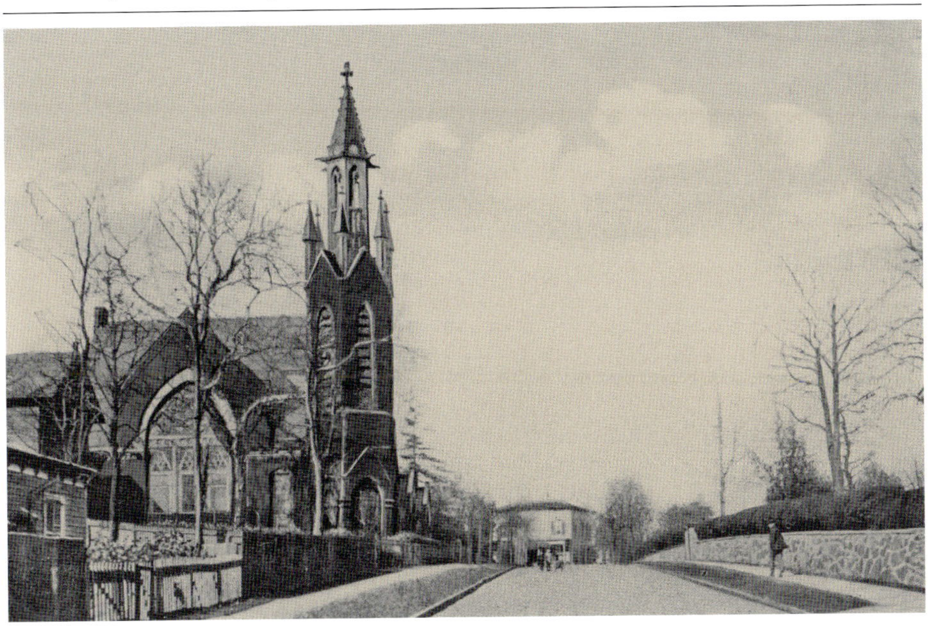

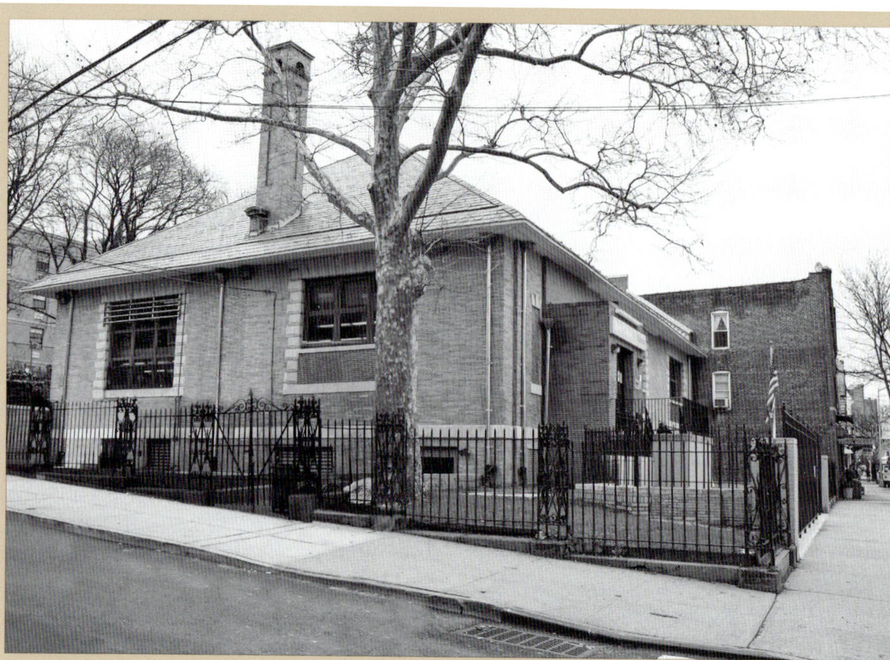

Steel tycoon Andrew Carnegie gave most of his fortune to charities. One favorite project was the Carnegie Foundation's library building program. The foundation would build a free library if a community could offer a location and make a commitment to fill the building with books. In 1902, St. George's church burned down at the northeast corner of Astoria Boulevard and 14th Street, and the location was offered for the library. The building was expanded over the years. (Then photograph courtesy Gary Vollo.)

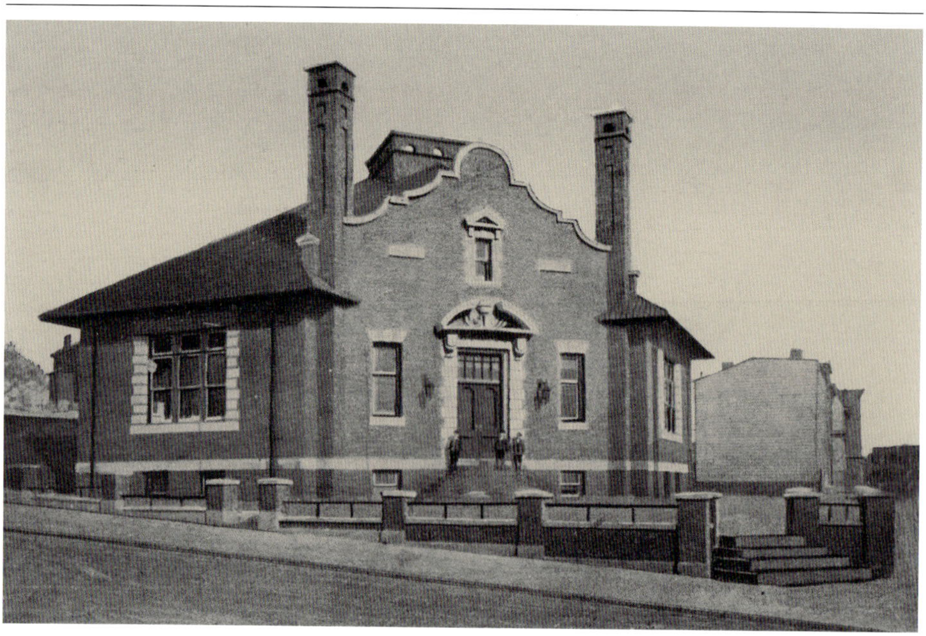

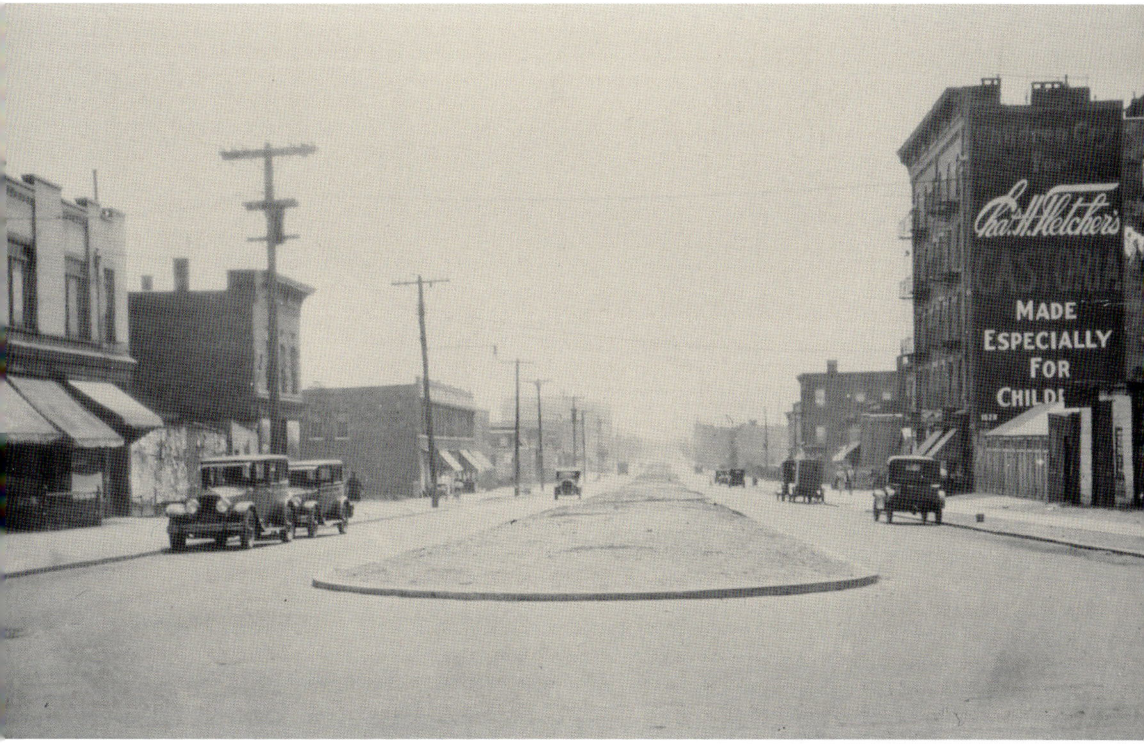

Called first Emerald Street from the large number of Irish who lived nearby, then Van Alst Street after a local landowner, 21st Street had a large median in its middle for a few blocks just south of Astoria Boulevard. The broad but uneven street was driven through the quagmire of Sunswick Creek, a former marsh that discouraged development until recently. (Then photograph courtesy Vincent Seyfried.)

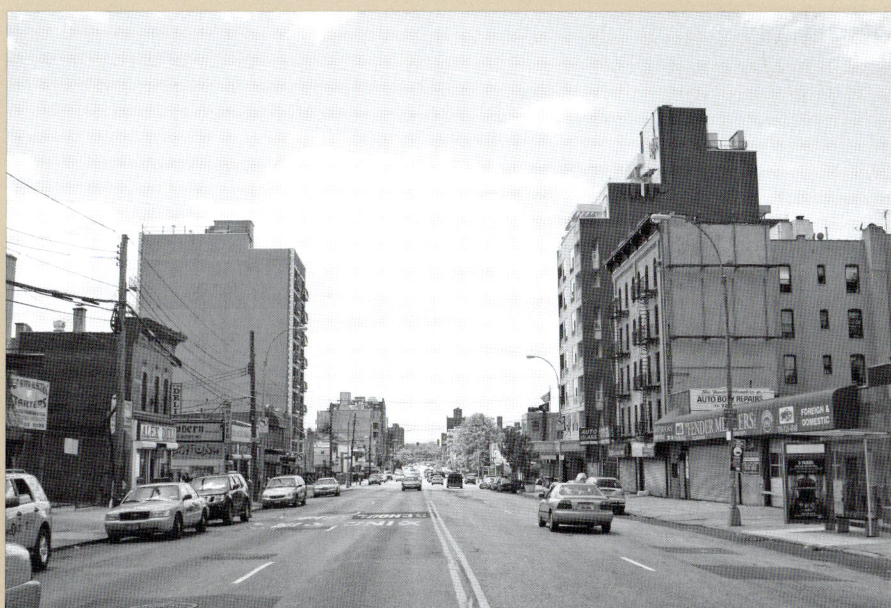

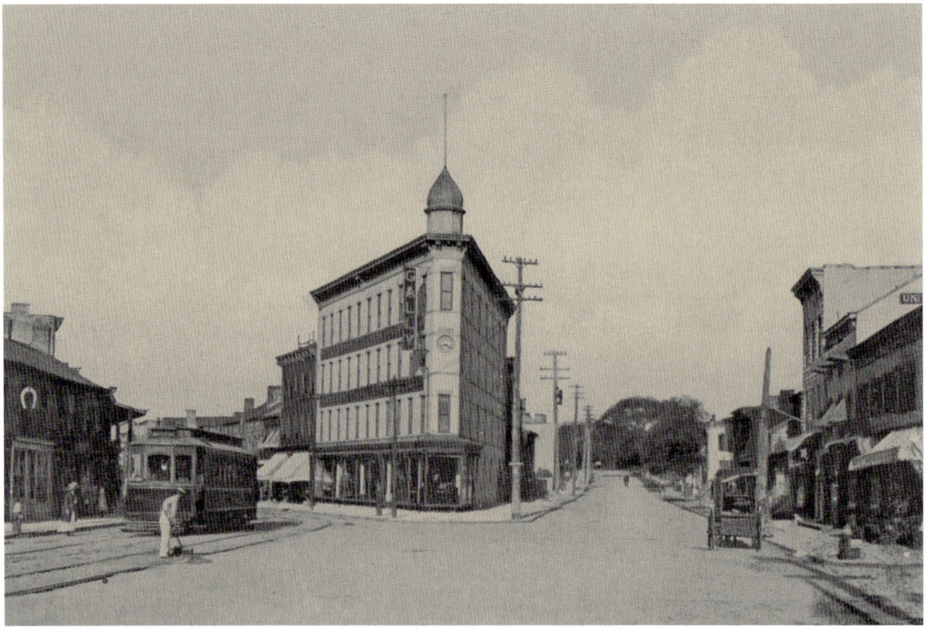

The triangular Astoria "Flatiron Building," at Astoria Square in Old Astoria, is just west of 21st Street. It is familiar to most in the community and is visible as far away as from the elevated train platform on Hoyt Avenue. Built about 1890, it replaced Albert Moritz's saloon, shown on page 67. The building has been home to furniture stores throughout most of its history. Astoria Boulevard is to the left, and Franklin (today 27th) Avenue on the right. (Then photograph courtesy Gary Vollo.)

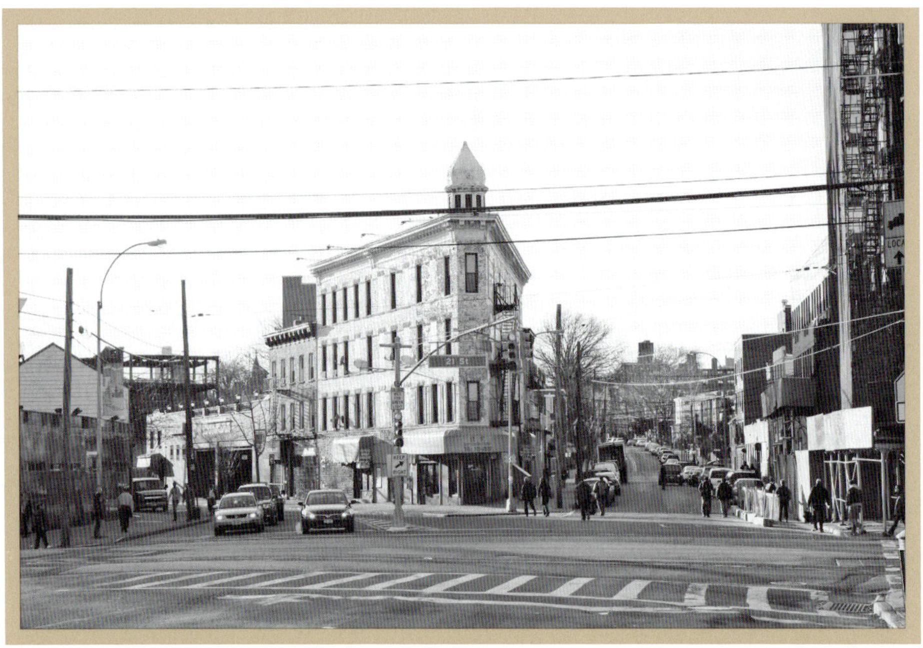

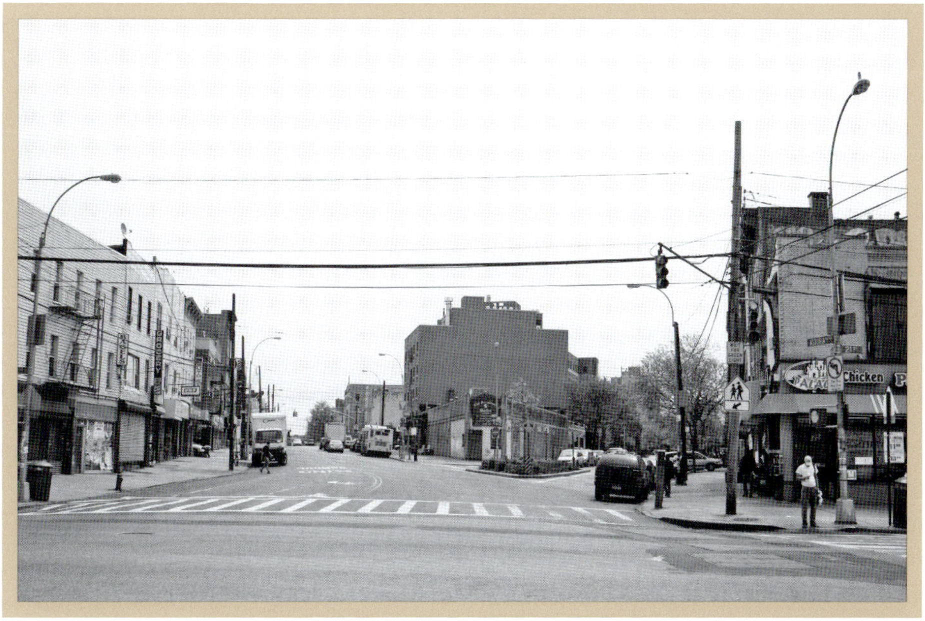

A second Astoria "Flatiron Building" stood at Andersen Square, a mirror of Astoria Square but just to the east of 21st Street. On Astoria Boulevard (to the left) was the Queens County Athletic Club, and in the distance was the tower from the parish school of Mount Carmel. To the right, on Newtown Avenue, Kerns Hotel and Summer Garden were next to Our Lady of Mount Carmel Church. Andersen was a dance hall proprietor at North Beach amusement park. (Then photograph courtesy Gary Vollo.)

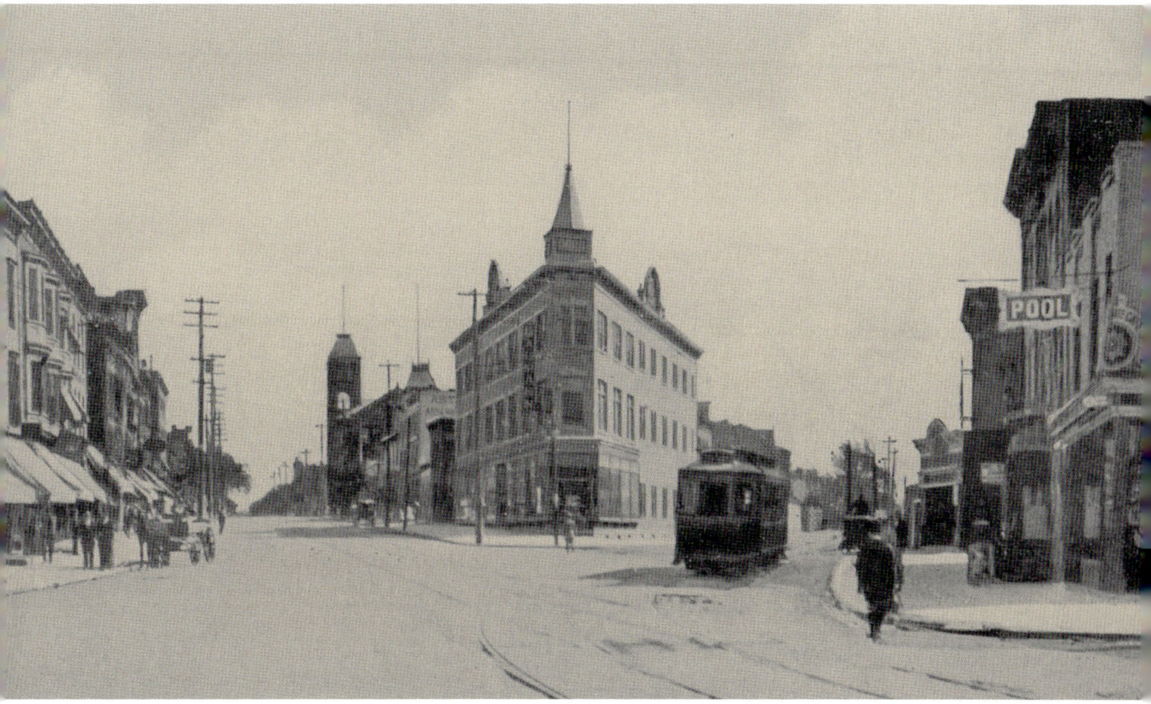

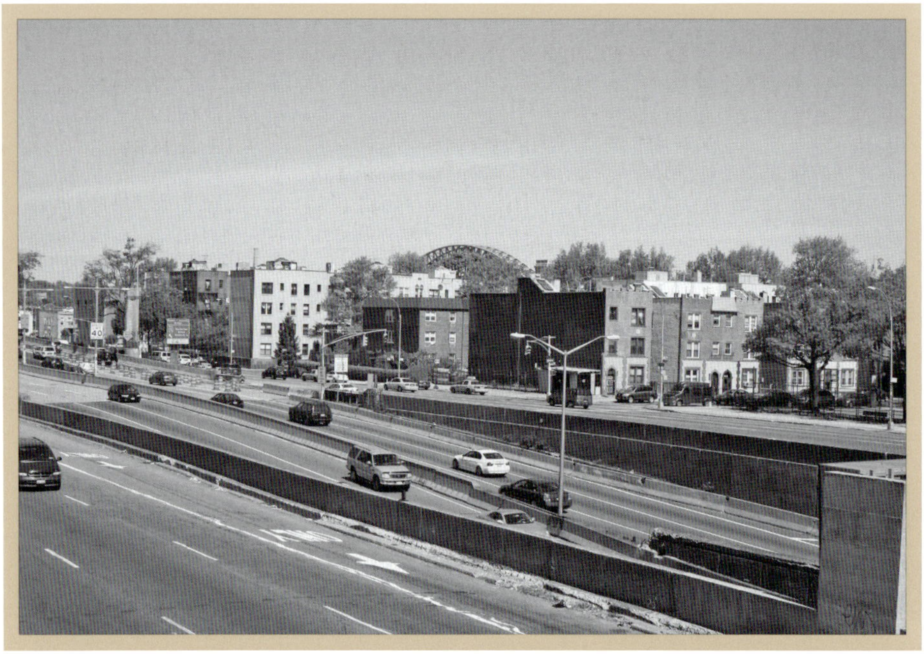

Robert Moses, the controversial urban planner, built highways that ripped apart older communities in Brooklyn and the Bronx—actions that are debated to this day. The Triborough (Robert F. Kennedy) Bridge ramp ran through Queens and obliterated a number of blocks in its path, including this stretch of 25th Avenue. Both views are from the elevated train platform at Hoyt Avenue. (Then photograph courtesy the Queens Borough Public Library–Long Island Division, Eugene L. Armbruster Photographs.)

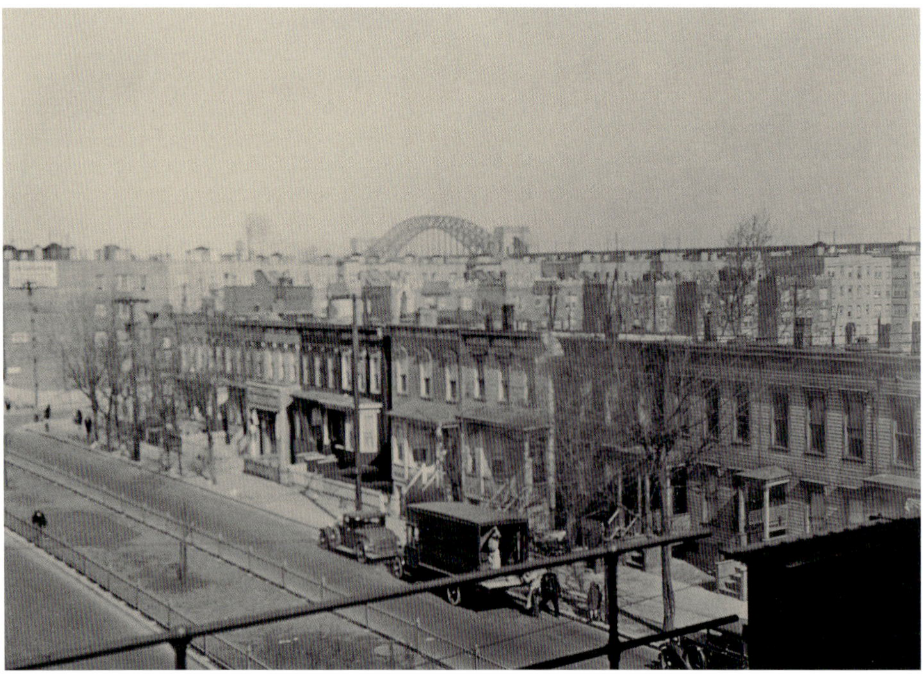

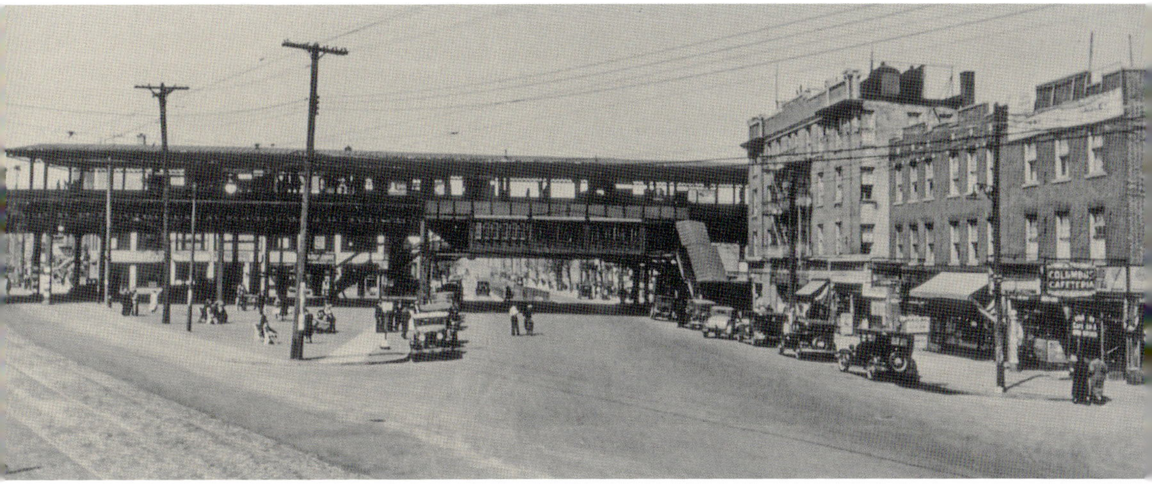

Transportation networks have played a big role in shaping the community. They have brought Long Island City into existence and divided it, as in the case of the Sunnyside Yards and Grand Central Parkway. This panoramic photograph of Columbus Square documents the wrenching changes brought about by the expressway, which demolished all buildings on the right. The elevated platform at Hoyt Avenue had to be nearly doubled to carry pedestrians over a noisy, polluting six-lane highway. The intersection is widely regarded as one of the most dangerous in the community.

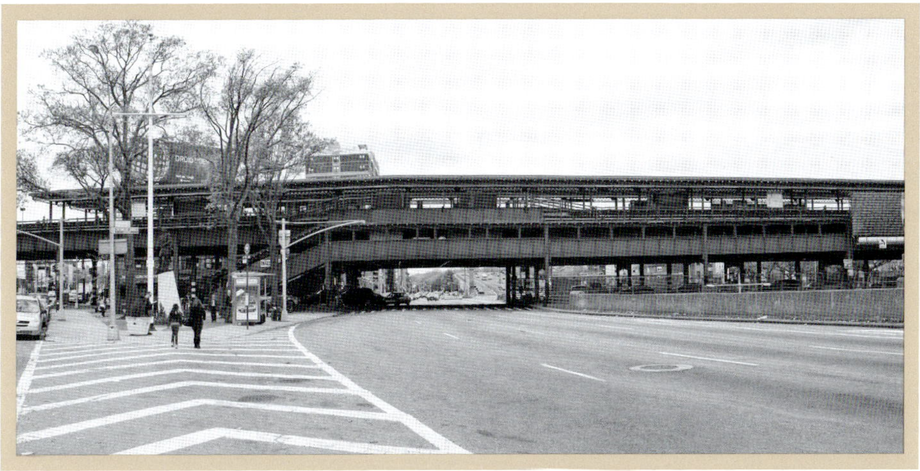

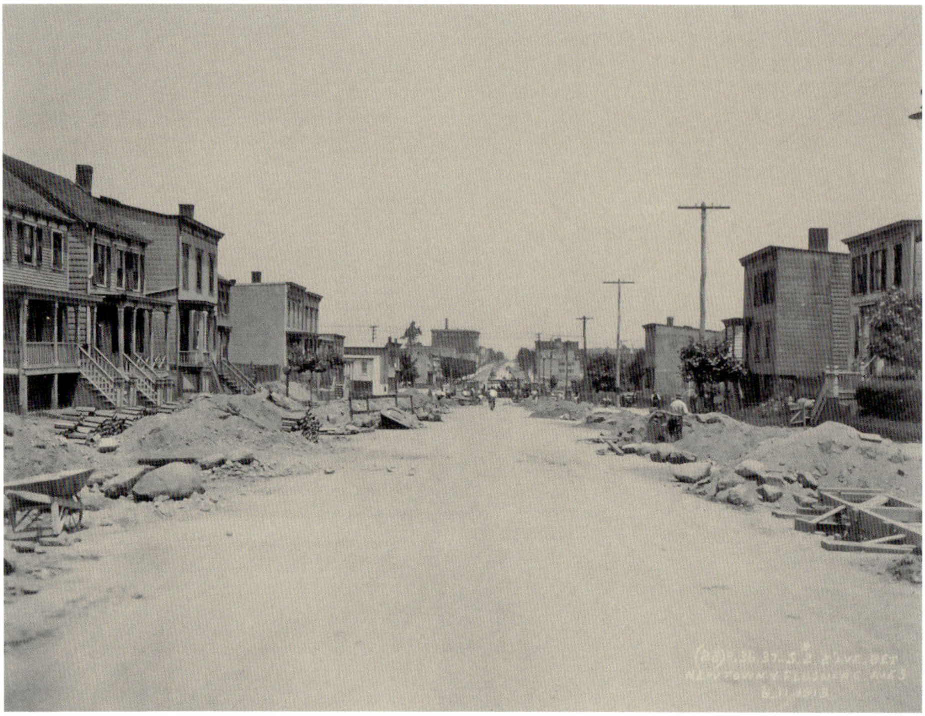

As it went through blocks that were all but empty, widening 31st Street to accommodate the newly elevated line was fairly easy. However, one notable hurdle had to be overcome—the built-up section near Astoria Boulevard. In this 1913 photograph looking north on 31st Street from Newtown Avenue towards Astoria Boulevard, dozens of older buildings that were jutting out into the right of way are pictured. They had to be either moved or cleared. In the background is P.S. 85 (1906).

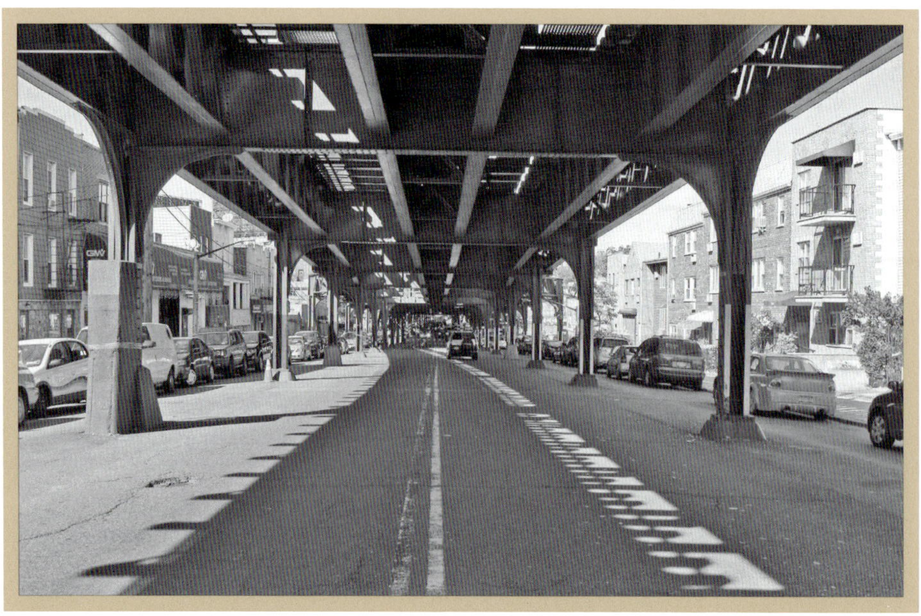

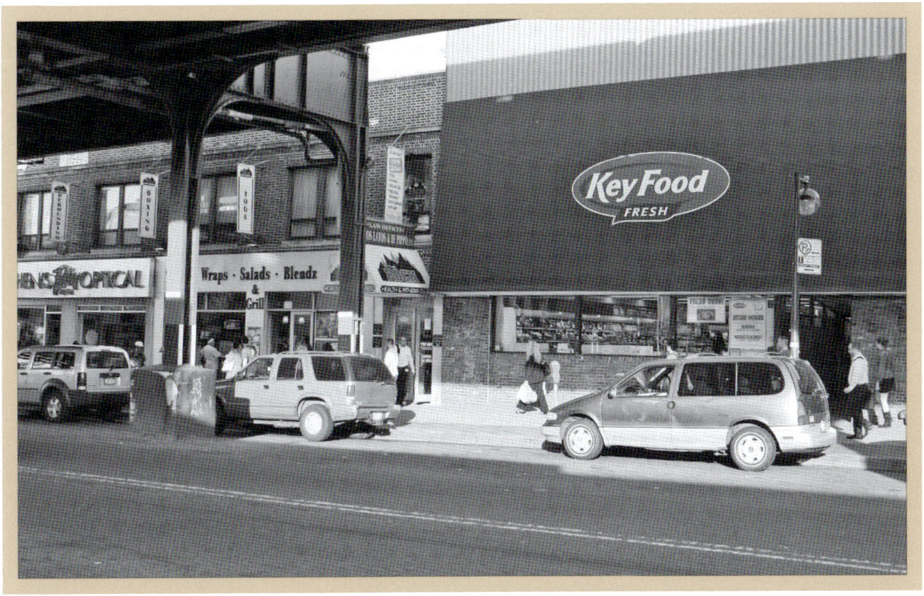

The Astoria Grand, a large theater seating 2,100, was on 31st Street off Ditmars Boulevard. It opened in 1924 and was closed in 1960. The building is now a supermarket. Over a dozen movie houses ensured that every neighborhood had a theater. With one exception, they have been replaced by one large multiscreen theater in western Queens. In recent years, showing movies in both museums and parks is bringing back a hint of the neighborhood theater. (Then photograph courtesy Henry Z. Steinway.)

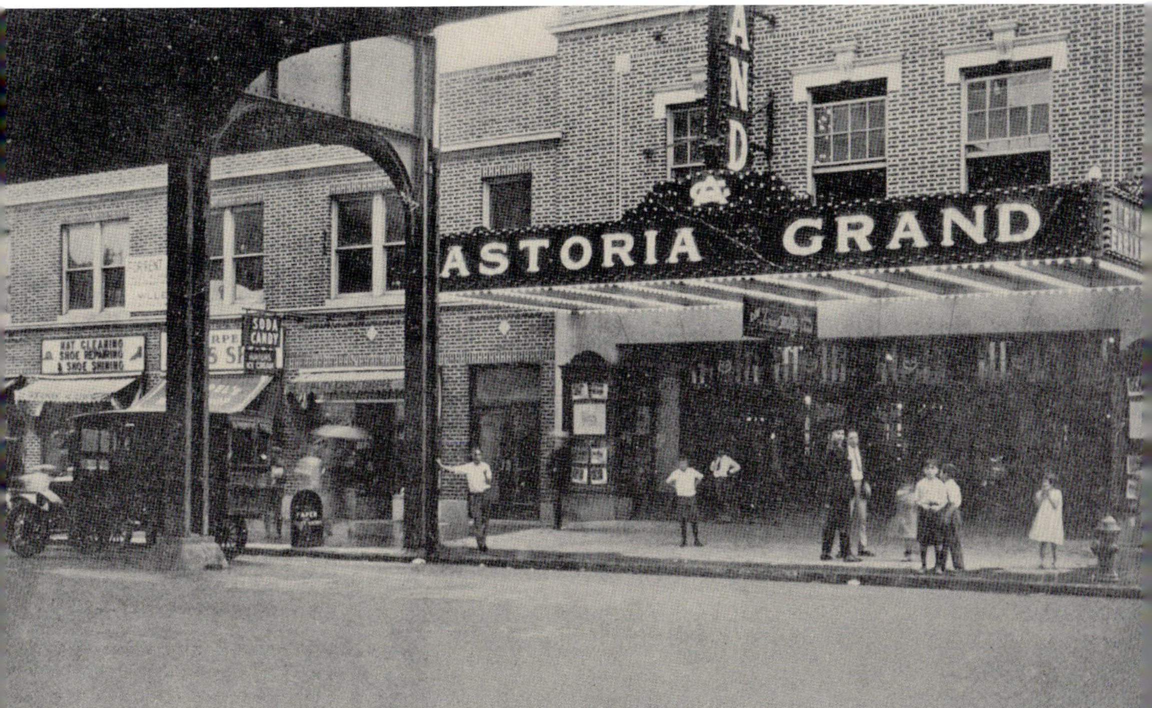

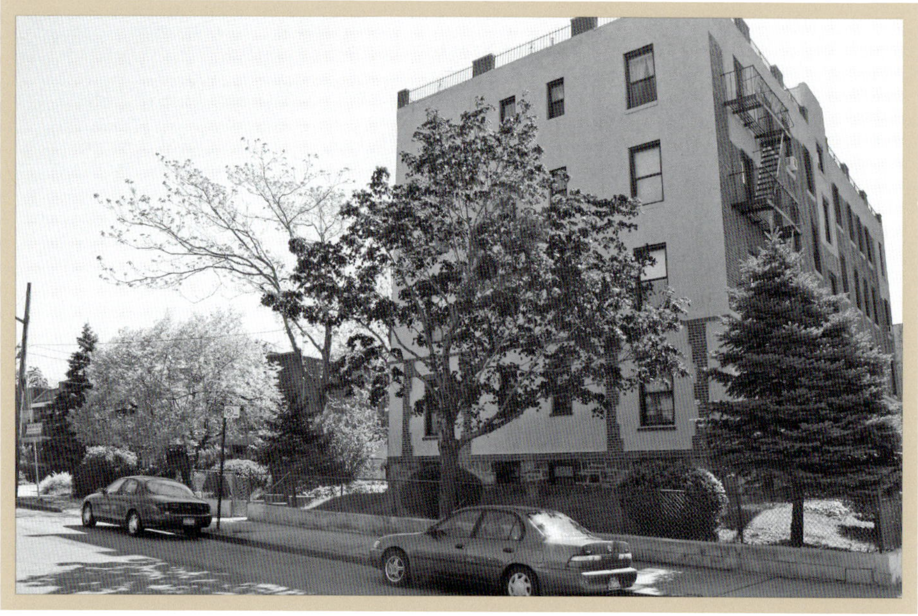

At the northeast corner of Ditmars Boulevard and Shore Boulevard was the Dr. Dow Ditmars house. Dr. Ditmars, who bought it in 1816, lived there until his death in 1860 at age 90. The square brick mansion with broad piazzas was the birthplace of Long Island City's first mayor, Abram D. Ditmars. In the background is the *c.* 1840 Rapalye-Polhemus mansion, whose cemetery is described on page 68. This building still stands near Shore Boulevard.

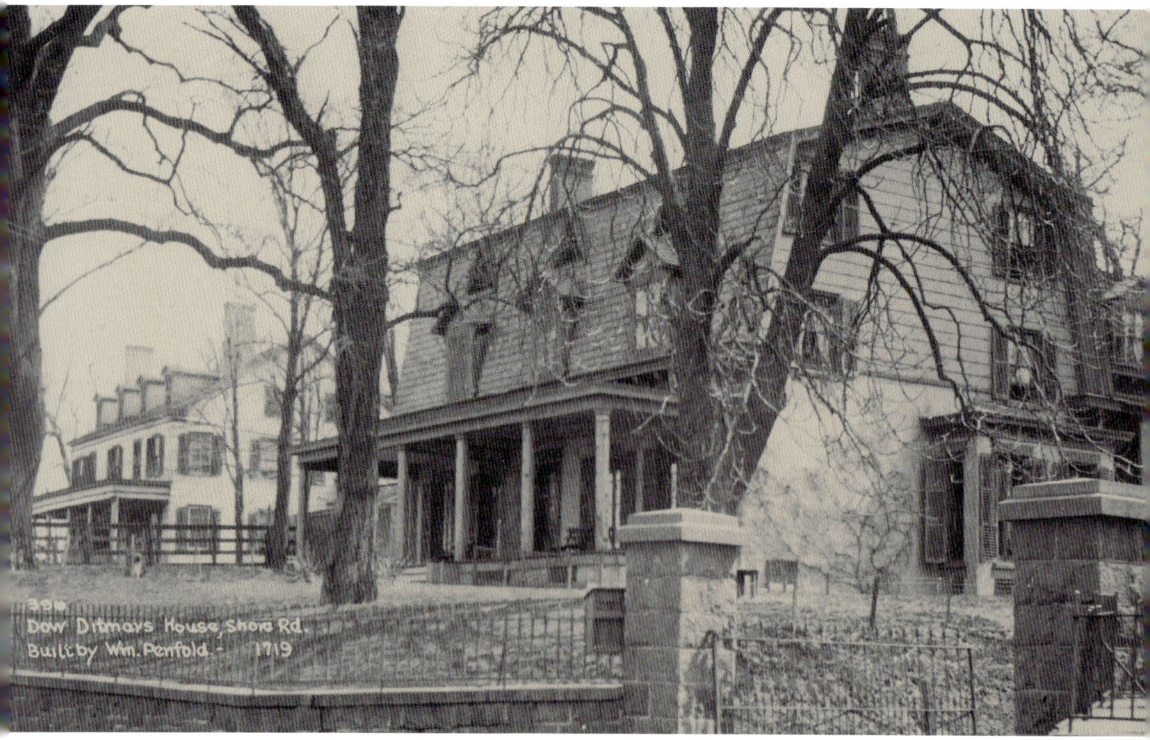

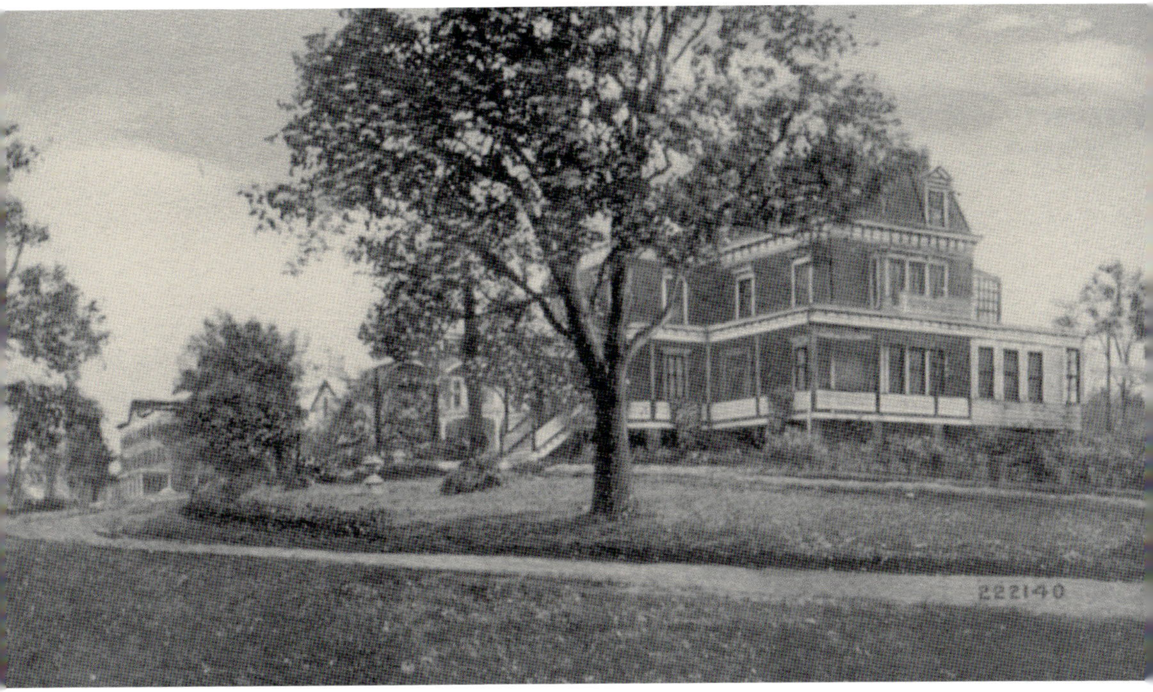

Frederick H. Wolcott was president of a dry goods company. He bought 30 acres on Shore Boulevard and in 1852 built a beautiful house (called The Hill) and personally designed its grounds. Dr. John Kindred purchased the estate in 1896 and turned it into the River Crest Sanitarium, catering to nervous diseases, alcoholism, and drug addiction. The property was broken apart for development, but the grounds around the mansion on Crescent Street remained intact. This is now St. John's Preparatory School.

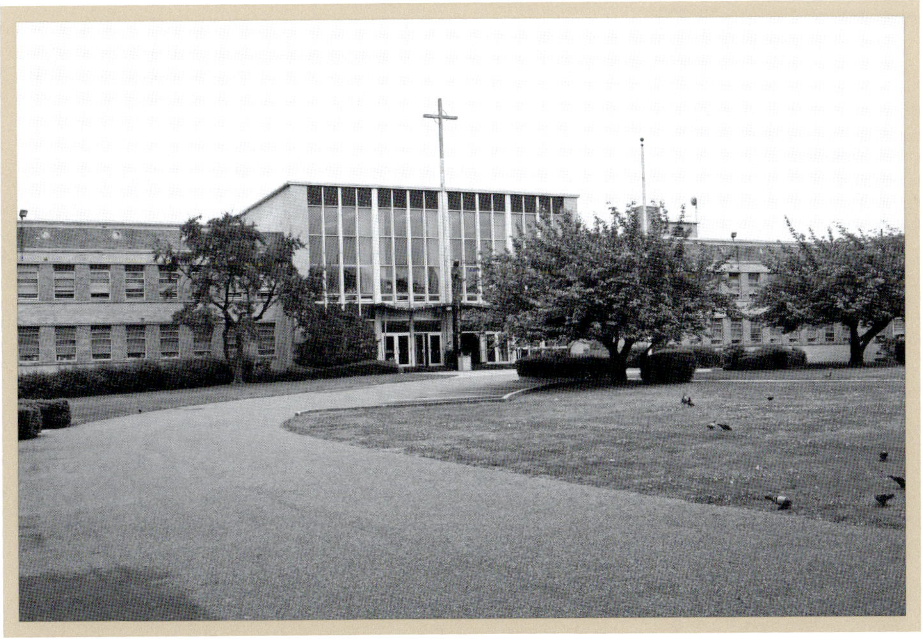

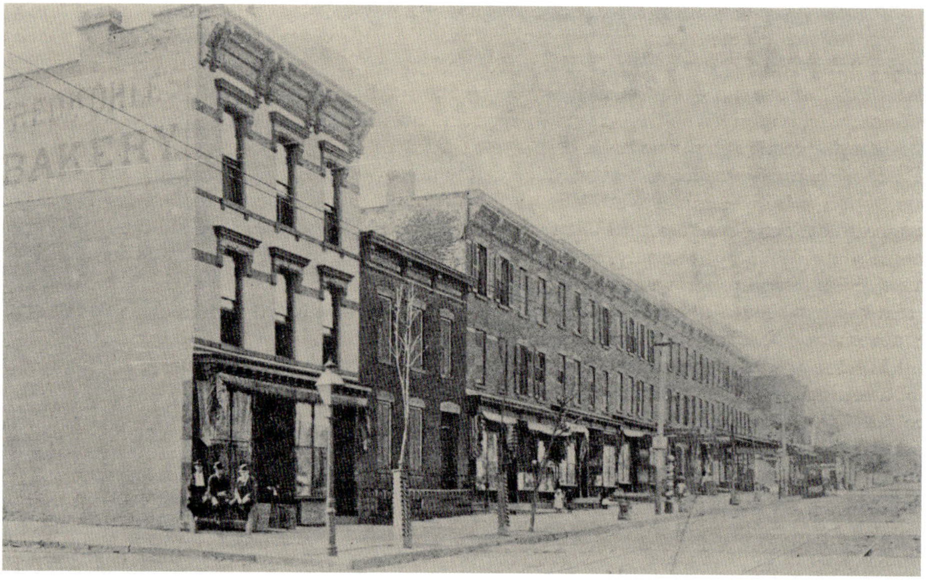

When the Steinway family looked at Long Island City in the late 1860s, they found cheap water transportation and room for expansion along the East River. The settlement was also far enough away from Manhattan to avoid the strikes and riots that disrupted their business and characterized urban life at that time. Their streetcar network linked the property to the wider region, making it a great opportunity for real estate speculation. These stores (around 1880) were built near 20th Road on Steinway Street.

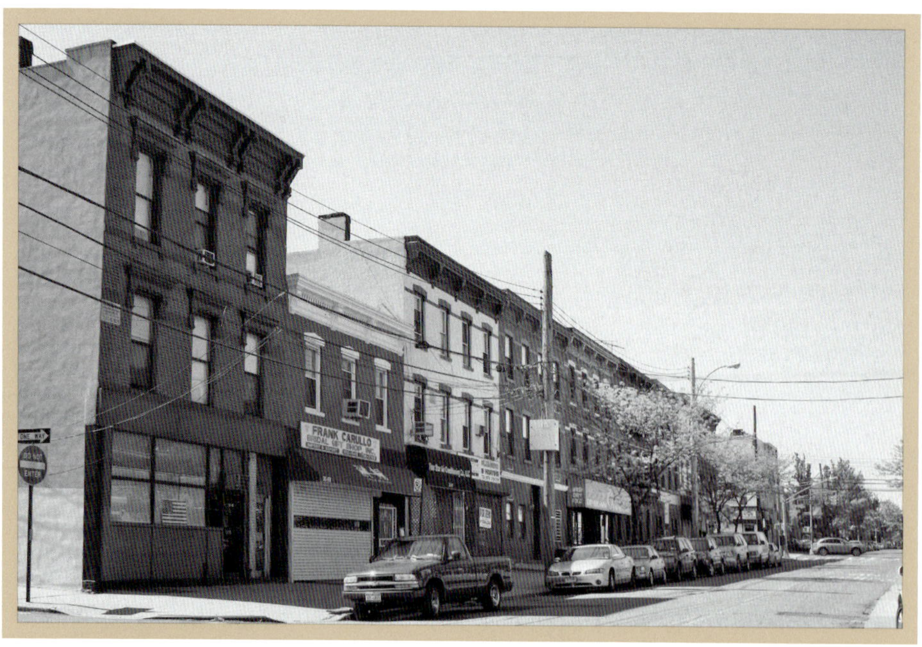

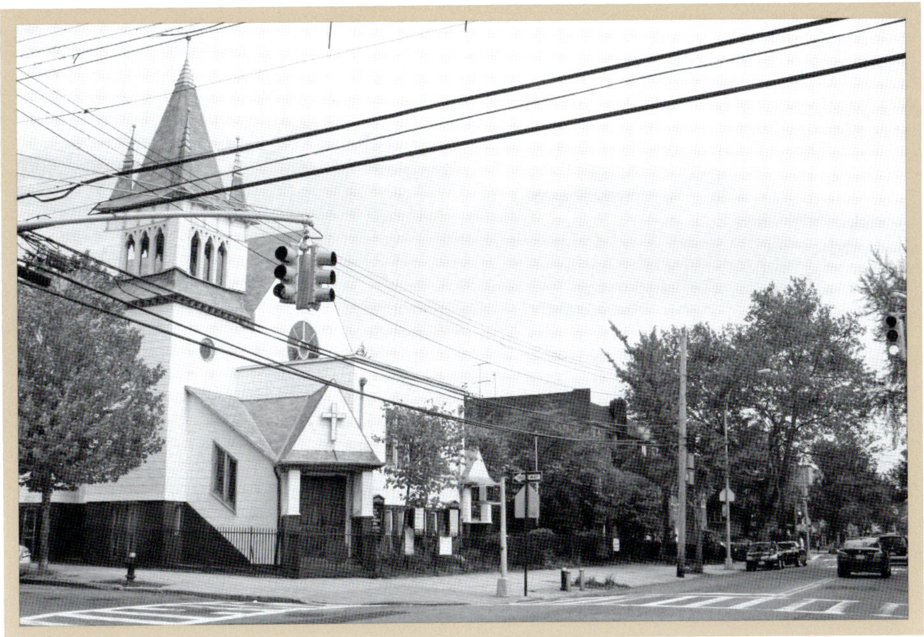

The Steinway Settlement was not a company town, since amenities such as churches, schools, a library, a kindergarten, and a park were open to both employees and local residents. In the 1950s, the Steinways were still selling off lots. As with Old Astoria Village, the community would benefit from an inventory of the historic structures within the company's 400-acre purchase. The Steinway Reformed Church (1891), at the corner of 41st Street and Ditmars Boulevard, once received a pipe organ from Steinway Hall in New York.

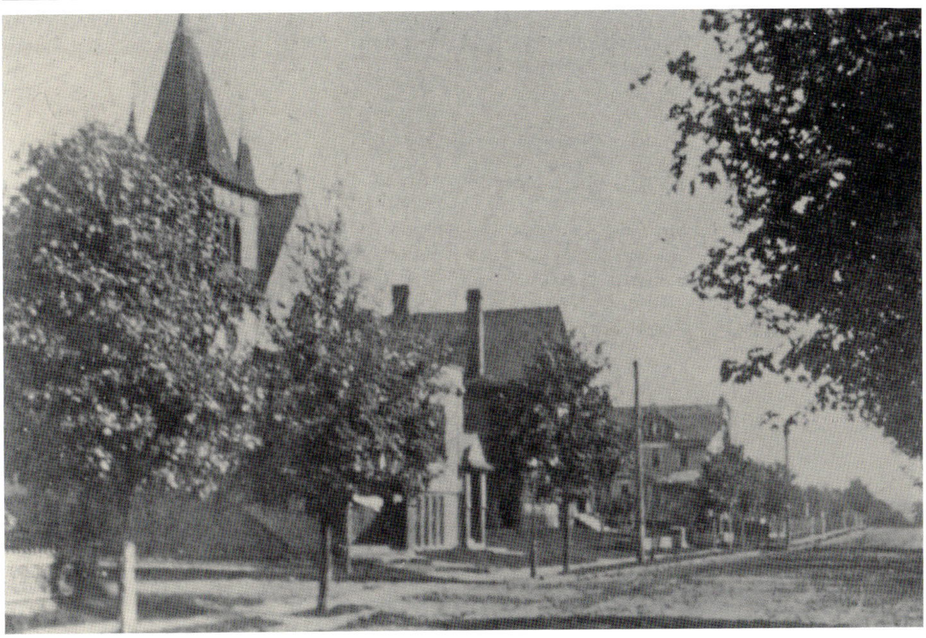

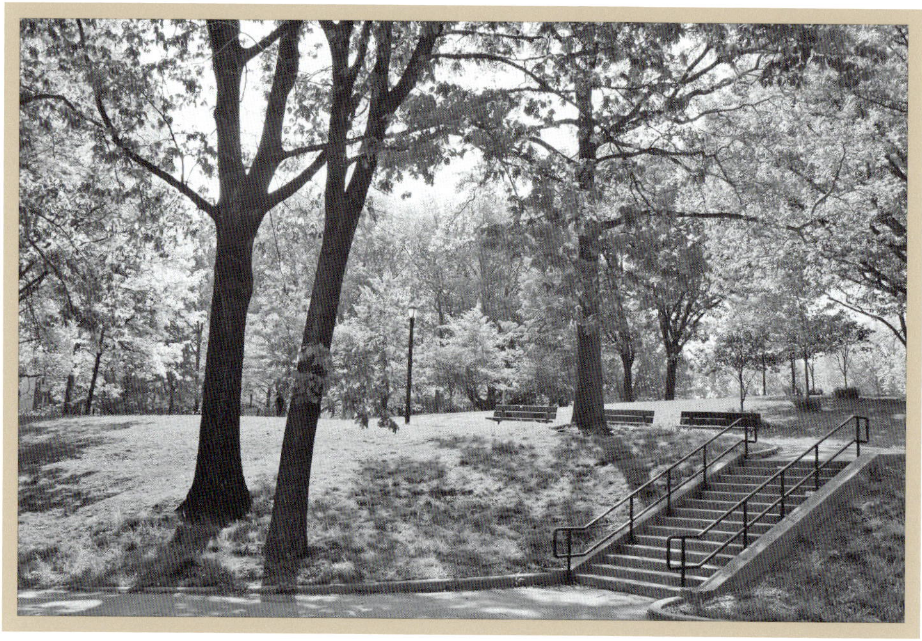

The Barclay Mansion (1840) stood in today's Astoria Park several hundred feet back from the river. It was typical of the great mansions that lined the East River for a few decades. It was torn down to make room for the Hell Gate Bridge abutments in 1914. Col. Thomas Barclay was the British consul general, and his sons, who started a countinghouse on Wall Street, were agents for Lloyds of London.

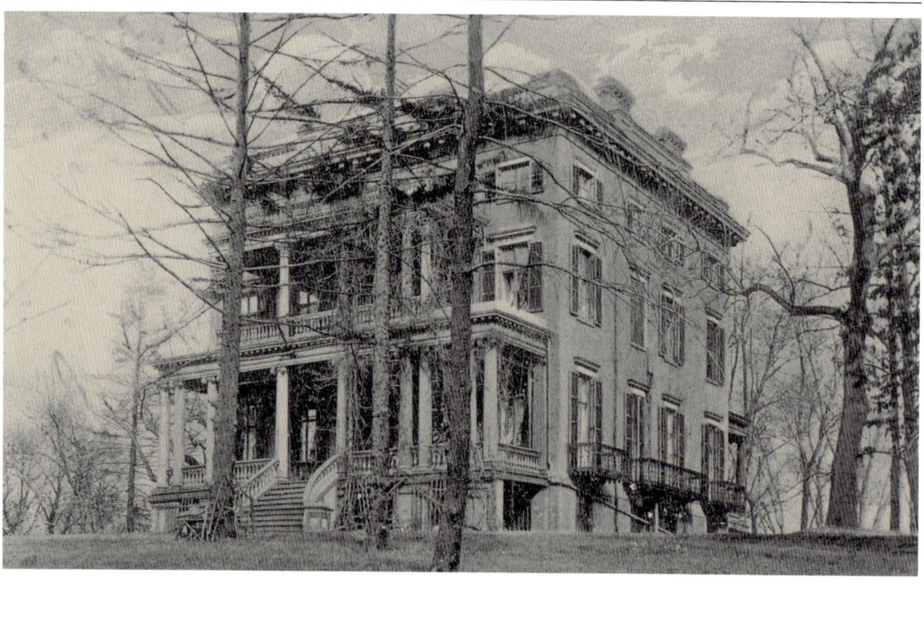

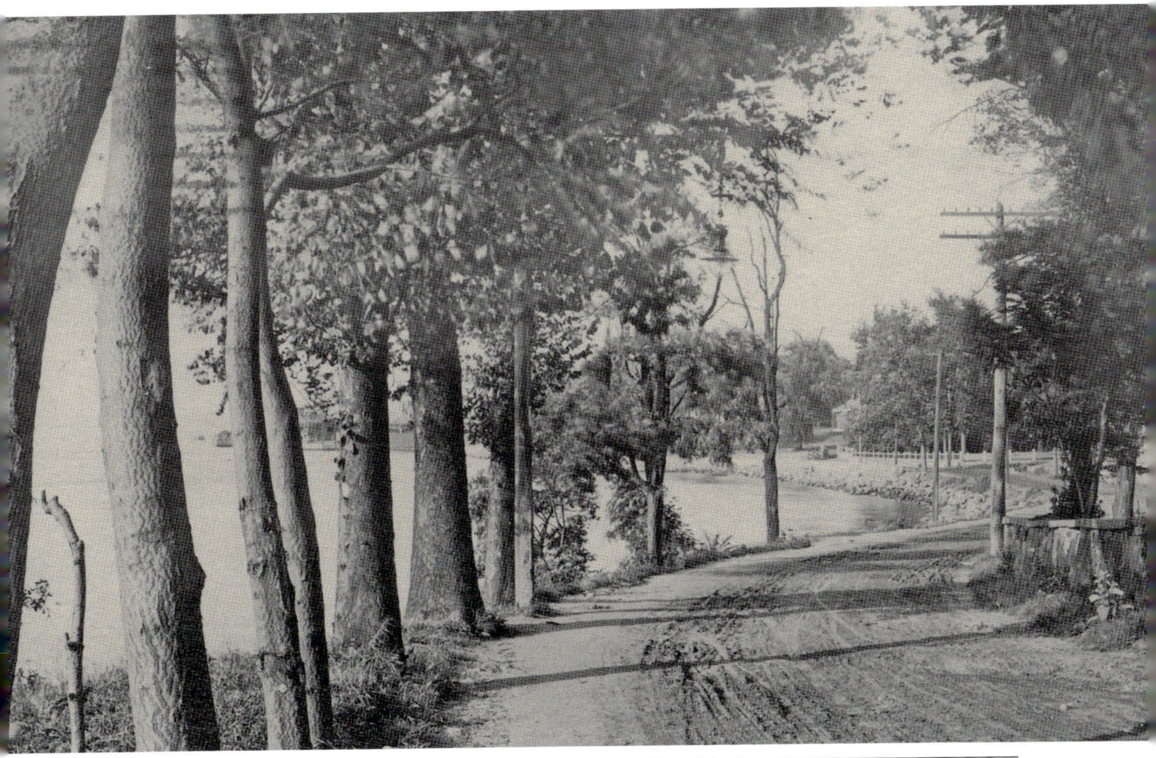

Shore Boulevard dates from colonial times and was a private lane used by wealthy families whose country houses lined the shore. Every estate contributed to maintaining a stone wall that once lined the road. Several private piers used to jut into the water, with remnants still visible today. In 1913, the city acquired more than 56 acres along the river for a park and officially named it Astoria Park that December.

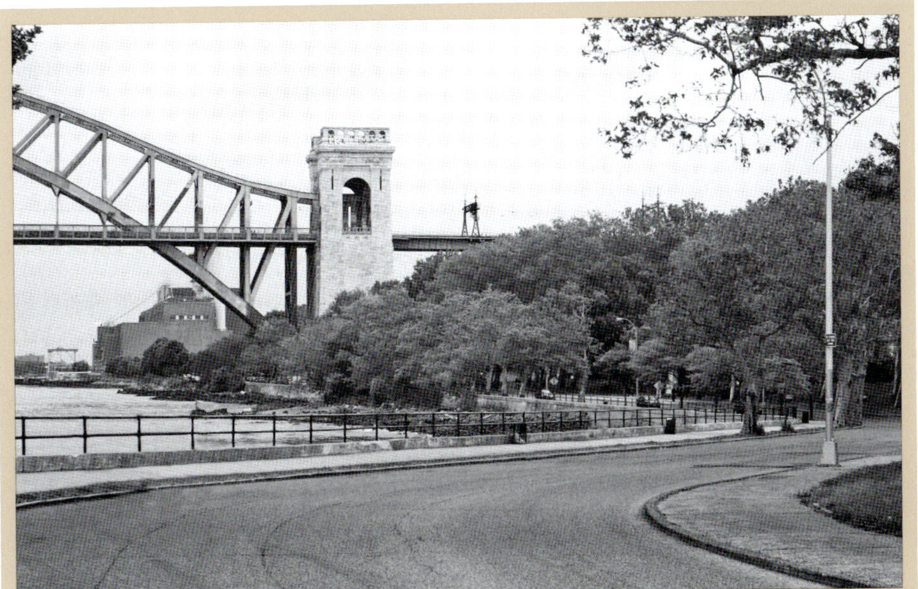

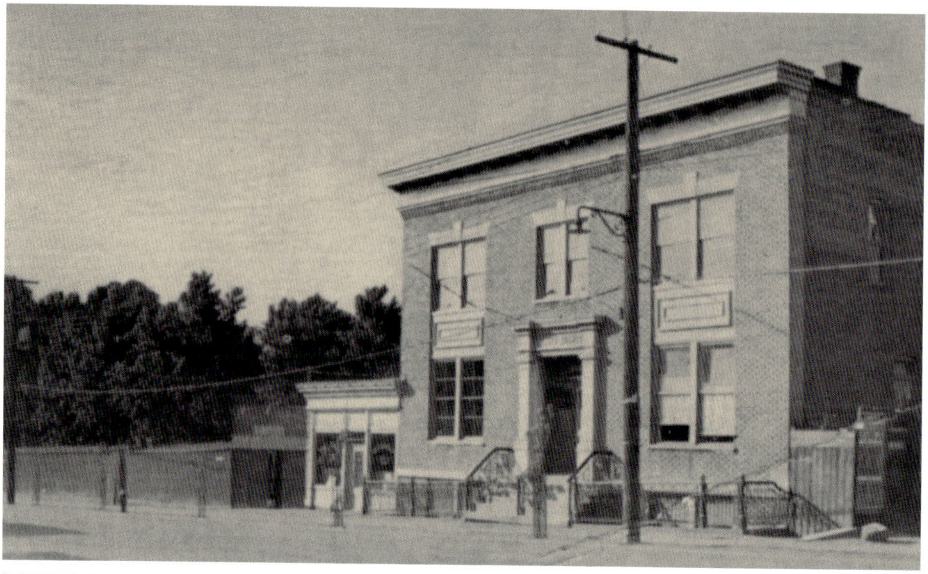

Long Island City has traditionally been home to new immigrant communities, who created fraternal groups and benevolent societies (such as the Bohemian Citizens' Benevolent Society of Astoria) to preserve the cultural life of the homeland and assist the newly arrived. For 100 years, Bohemian Hall and Beer Garden has been important to the community. Carved over the building's entrance is the phrase *Český Domov*, meaning "Czech Home." Today everyone is at home in Bohemian Hall and Park. (Then photograph courtesy Bohemian Citizens' Benevolent Society of Astoria.)

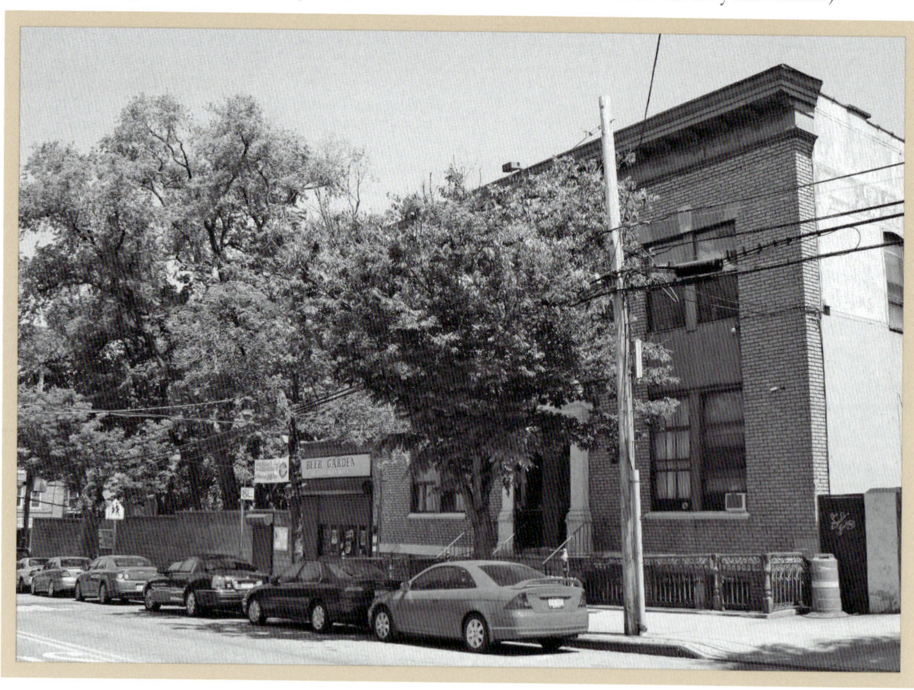

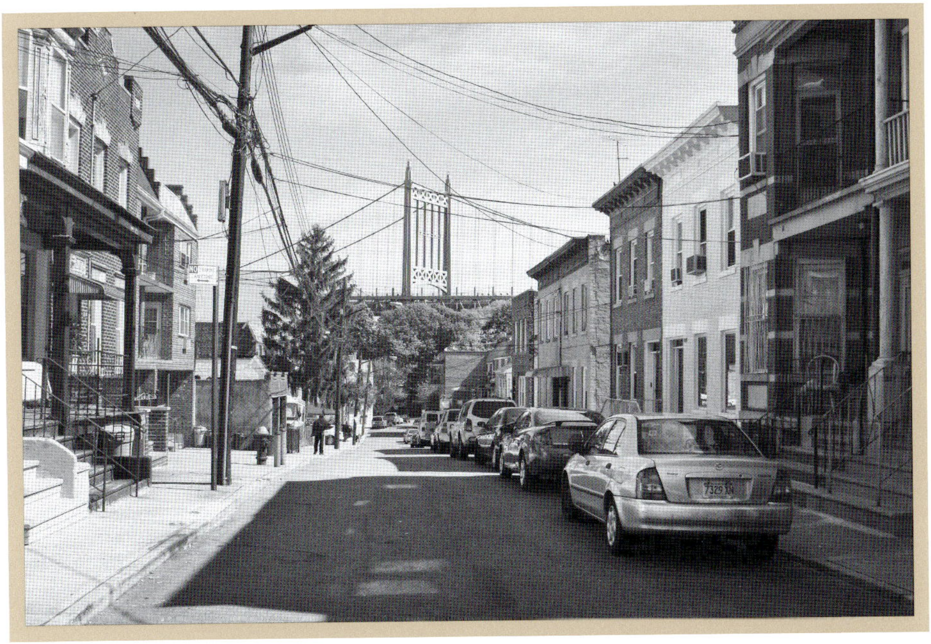

This block characterizes things that make the community special: enduring traditions of a familiar neighborhood juxtaposed with a world of promise and beauty symbolized by the distant bridges. Long Island City and its communities existed long before anyone now living, and, as is the kinetic nature of places, will change and benefit generations yet unborn. It is a place for people to find a home and to reach out and touch the American Dream.

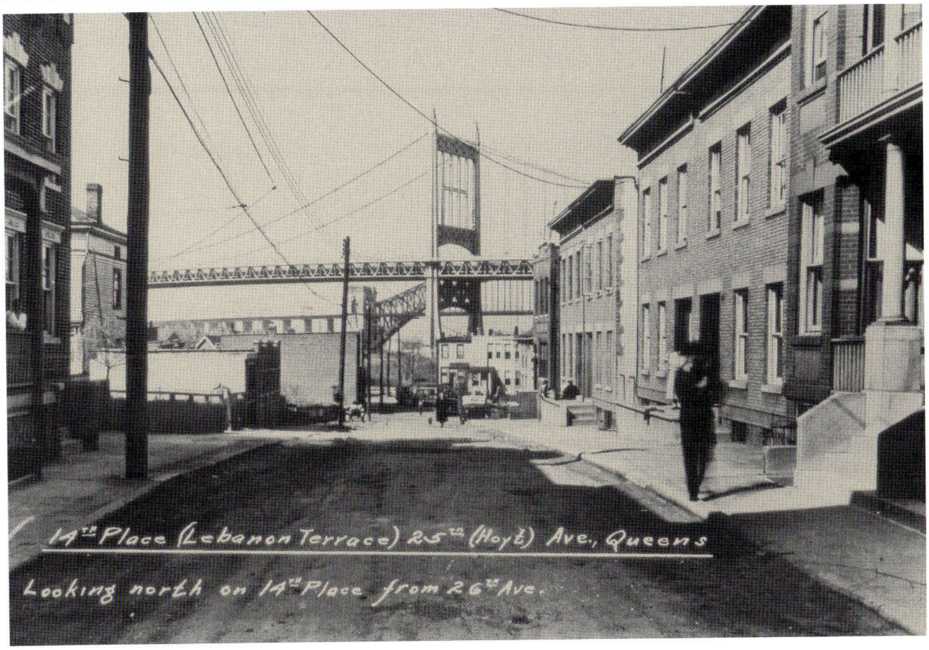

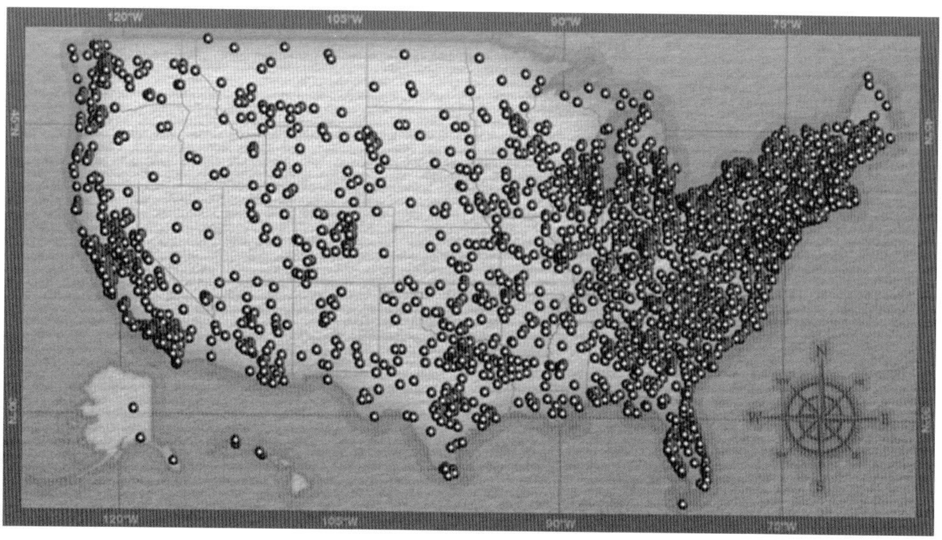